THE
BALCONINNY

Let school-taught pride dissemble all it can,
These little things are great to little man;
And wiser he whose sympathetic mind
Exults in all the good of all mankind. . . .
—THE TRAVELLER

The
Balconinny

By

J. B. PRIESTLEY

Harper & Brothers Publishers

NEW YORK AND LONDON

1931

The Balconinny

Copyright, 1930, by J. B. Priestley

Printed in the U. S. A.

SECOND PRINTING

D—F

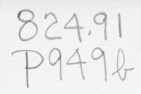
CONTENTS

《 V 》

CONTENTS

THE
BALCONINNY

THE BALCONINNY

ONE of my ambitions has been realized at last. For the past two months we have been living at the very edge of the sea and—this is the point—are the temporary owners of what the youngest member of this family, a neologist of something like genius, calls a 'balconinny.' If you saw it you would see at once that it is a balconinny rather than a balcony, being just large enough to hold three comfortably seated people. You could have tea on it—at a pinch—but not lunch or dinner. There is only room for one bed. If this is not a balconinny, then what is it?

You can slip out of either the drawing-room or the best bedroom on to this balconinny. I never fail to enjoy the thrill of it, for I have always wanted to have a balcony overlooking the sea—and here it is, even though it is only a balconinny. There is always something dramatic and heart-lifting about the contrast. One moment you are in the drawing-room, which is full of mysterious water-colours and little tables that must not be touched; or you are in the best bedroom, which is

« 1 »

full of enormous wardrobes and photographs of people you don't know; and the very next moment you are a thousand miles away from such things, looking at the sea and sky. It is true there is a road or promenade below, but you need never notice that; look straight ahead, or for that matter to left or right—anywhere, in fact, but downwards—and you might think you were on a ship, a large, steady, clean ship. Staying here, indeed, is a sea-voyage artfully shorn of its disadvantages, the rust-coloured bath water and the stewed tea, the miseries of bunkdom, and such problems as ' Does the cabin steward really deserve more than the dining-room steward?' I have done eight thousand miles at sea and found less to look at than I find here in a single afternoon.

Moreover, we overlook no common waters. This is the corner of England where everything except woad-painting and cairn-building began, for here Julius himself beached his ships and Augustine landed. These are the Downs where the old merchantmen and men-o'-war found an anchorage. Out there are the Goodwins, which are lighted like a park every night. If you want an atmosphere of wrecks and lifeboats (did I not first make the acquaintance of this place in the heroic pages of *Chatterbox*, ages ago?) and smuggler and pigtails and tarry trousers, haunted by the ghost of a jolly lyric by Charlie Dibdin, then this is the place for you.

Not that we have to amuse ourselves here by dreaming of the past—a miserable business. Something is always happening, here and now. You never know what will be conjured on to this shining mirror. The other night, returning from a day in London, a long hot dusty futile day, which can only be compared with that of a mite revisiting the interior of a large cheese, I saw in the blue hollow of sea and sky two white yachts lying out there, close together, like two mysterious beautiful ladies whispering together and idly flashing their jewels; and when I rushed out on to the balcony, early next morning, these yachts had gone, stolen away, and I half wondered if I had dreamt them. But that very morning, in came a Dutch mine-layer or mine-sweeper, looking like the fat brother of that French Fisheries boat we had seen a few days before. And this is to say nothing of the regular traffic of this magic street: the great P. & O. and Union-Castle liners, the tankers and grain-ships and tramps and tiny coasting steamers, the brigs and luggers and little racing yachts.

Sometimes we take the day's papers on to the balcony, but we find it hard to give them any serious attention; their politicians and millionaires and criminals and bright young people are only the vaguest of spectres; and soon, so soon—as Shakespeare might have said—their gaudy, babbling and remorseful day has crept into the bosom of the sea.

When I looked out from the balcony this morning, there was neither day nor sea, just vaguely shining space, as if we were hanging over the world's edge. The hooting of the invisible lightship might have come from some doomed star. We breakfasted on the very margin of all substantial things. More light stole through, and in place of that vast nothing there was so much shimmering silk, grey below and palest blue above, and on this fabric were tiny moving shapes, delicate as moths, yet most of them, it may be, crammed with fish and iron bars and bales of cotton, full of men making stew or smoking cut plug. To-morrow morning, if the glass falls and the wind freshens, there will not be a trace of all this ghostliness. The horizon will have come back again, a long green line, broken into a white jumble here and there where the Goodwins set the water creaming. The whole flood will be running stormily at us, smashing at the shingle, throwing handfuls of salt into the whistling air, and churning round the ships, now as hard and clear to sight as black paint and red paint can make them. And the whole place will look as if the sea had washed all over it during the night, for everything will be clean and have a salty sparkle. What a show to have a private box for, a box you can use any time of day! Even Mr. Cochrane must admit his defeat. He has his dancers, but what did Prince Florizel cry? 'When you do dance, I wish you a wave o' the sea, that you might ever do nothing but that.' And here they do nothing but that.

Perhaps the best time of all is after dinner, especially on these warm and windless nights, when you can take one of those glorious long cheroots out on the balcony and watch the ash reach its third half-inch. You can also watch for some of the last signs of picturesque romance left to this world. Last night I was up there, when it was nearly dusk, and saw far out, nearly on the horizon, a full-rigged ship. And that is by no means an everyday affair, seeing a full-rigged ship. But that was not all. Somewhere an artist was at work. The house, the promenade, the foreshore, were all settling into dusk, and the sea itself was fading and darkening; but out there, where the ship was, the last gleams of sunset were falling, and for a minute or two she was irradiated, and even when her hull was no longer flushed, her great sails were still golden, and even when they paled and sank, her masts still seemed tangled with the unset. Then, in the deeper dusk, she turned ghostly, and at last she vanished, just flitted away when our heads were turned, like a ghost. Perhaps she was a ghost.

The lights of the Goodwins came twinkling on, a little uncertainly at first, as if they were not quite sure they were wanted. Away on the right, the pier put on its little coloured spangle of lights, which dropped long trembling reflections into the water. On the cliff to the left our neighbouring town turned itself into a bracelet of glimmering yellow points. The whole traffic of the sea became a pattern of lights, fixed or wandering, in a mystery of purple air and indigo waters. You saw something that looked like a distant row of houses on the move and you knew that a liner from Calcutta or the Cape had passed by and that hundreds of your fellow-countrymen were staring over the rails and hearing the great

engines go humming, *Home-in-the-morning,
Home-in-the-morning*. And little lights, as lonely
as a few fireflies in a desert, crept by, going the
other way, and you knew that a tramp or two
had slipped out of the Thames, bound perhaps
for Monte Video or Callao.

These and many other things we saw last night,
as we sat on our little balcony. And our neighbours had set some works in motion in a box,
and out of this box there came some familiar and
great music, and in this music we saw Siegfried
and the dragon and the leaping fire and the deep
enchantment of the forest; and all this too flowed
easily into the night and was one with it. Long
after we have left this house I shall still use its
balcony. They will tell me this and that; they
will argue and fuss and sweat; they will point
out that Jones is overpraised and Smith under-
rated, that Brown should go out and Robinson
come in; and it will not matter; I shan't hear them.
I shall be back on this balconinny.

I AM one of the very few authors who have ever appeared with the Beecham Opera Company. It is true that I was not expected to sing—though I did sing. It is also true that I played with the Company for one night only. I was not asked to appear again, but then, on the other hand, I never asked to be asked again. Once was quite enough; I have no serious operatic ambitions; and now nobody can say I have never appeared in opera just as they cannot say I have never been to Africa; I have had my night with the Beecham Company just as I have had my half-day in Algiers.

The time is ten years ago, the spring of 1919. The place—a provincial city. I am newly returned from that dismal progression—heroics, endurance, boredom, disgust—known up to the present as the Great War. I am writing articles and reviews for the local paper at a guinea a column. In one of the principal streets of my city I encounter an old acquaintance of the ranks and we have what he calls, very inaccurately, 'a gill.' He tells me that this week he is assisting the Beecham Opera Company. I remember then that it is his practice to 'walk on' at the local theatres. I myself had seen him as an Eastern domestic, a policeman, member of a jury, a forester, and as the Bishop in *Richard the Third*. Indeed, it was a poor week at our Theatre Royal when he did not walk on as somebody or other, always dumb. Six of them, it appears, are walking on this very night in Gounod's *Romeo and Juliet*. This is one of the few operas for which I have not booked seats. I do not want to see *Romeo and Juliet*, but I should like to appear in it. I am even willing— so eager, so rash, are we amateurs—to hand over the night's pay, the whole two and sixpence, to the man whose place I take. The matter can be arranged. I am to be at the theatre at seven-thirty, to meet my acquaintance at the stage door.

I am there and he is there, and the two of us, with a last glance at the waiting crowds, march in through the stage door. We go up steps and down steps and along so many corridors that I am completely bewildered. At last we arrive at a dressing-room that is as hot as an oven—and well it might be, for it must be somewhere near the centre of the earth. The room contains one long mirror, several large theatrical baskets, an overpowering smell of grease paint, and one bored little man in his shirt-sleeves. There is a notice: *Smoking Strictly Prohibited*. We all light up at once, all, that is, except the little man, who was smoking when we entered and seems to have been smoking without cessation for about forty years. He opens one of the baskets, and begins throwing costumes at us.

I find myself wearing a yellow and black doublet or whatever it is, and one black tight and one striped yellow and black tight; and I look like a rather plump wasp. The little man takes our faces, one by one, and rubs red and brown into them. Then we put on brown or black wigs, thick and bobbed, and crown them with little round hats, Beefeater style. To complete our discomfort—for the wigs are very hot and the hats do not feel as if they were on—we are now given pikes about eight feet long. We are, it seems, the town guard of Verona, and I have no doubt we look the part or, indeed, something better than the part. We have all been in the army, and I will wager we could have mopped up the real town guard of Verona—and Vicenza and Padua—in a jiffy. But not, I must confess, with those pikes.

When an opera company as big as the Beecham concern is playing in a provincial theatre there is no room behind the scenes for a walking stick, let alone half a dozen eight-feet pikes. As we trail our pikes down steps and up steps and along corridors, we are cursed by Montagues and Capulets together. 'A plague on both your houses!' we mutter, trying in vain to disentangle ourselves.

We arrive in the wings. The opera has begun, but we are not wanted for some time. To walk into that brightly lit space looks a fearsome enterprise, yet we see fellows dashing on and off and never turning a hair. Mercuito—or some other bearded gallant—waves his arms and reaches a top note, then comes out into the wings and lights a cigarette. But now we are summoned. The stage manager has remarked our existence. He is the most worried-looking man I have ever seen. Everything he does appears to be one last desperate effort. Night after night he dies a hundred deaths. Now he seizes a pike and shows us how it should be carried.

Our duties, he explains, are simple. We make two appearances. The first time we march on, we stand, we march off. Nothing could be easier, though it is clear that as he says this he does

not believe we shall find it easy. He only means
that if this were the world he thought it was
when he first undertook stage management, it
would be easy. As it is, if we were to go pranc-
ing round the stage, tearing the scenery with our
pikes, he would not be really surprised. He alone
is sane in a lunatic world. Now comes a big scene.
More and more people crowd on to the stage and
make more and more noise. At last we are the
only performers left in the wings. Is it our turn
now? It is. Affairs in Verona are at a crisis. There
is nothing for it but to summon the town guard.
But will the town guard come? They will. At
this moment they are fearfully carrying their six
pikes in the tiny space between the drop and the
back wall of the theatre, to appear through a
central arch. There we were. No applause greeted
us; nobody paid much attention to us, either on
the stage or in the audience; but we did what we
had to do manfully. We marched on; we stood;
we marched off. Half the opera was saved. Back
in the wings I hear a thunder of applause, and I
wonder if the audience is aiming some of it at
us, if they are saying to one another, 'The princi-
pals and chorus are not very good, but the town
guard is magnificent, especially the third one with

the black tight.' What would happen if I insisted upon taking a curtain with Romeo and Juliet? I see myself standing between them, pike in hand, bowing gracefully. What I do, however, is to retire to our subterranean dressing-room with the other five. The little man is still there, sinking into a more profound boredom. He must have always been there. Perhaps the theatre was built round him.

It is almost time for our second and final appearance. We are back in the wings, and the stage manager, now far beyond hope, a man resigned to his fate in an idiotic universe, gives us our instructions. There is to be an admirable little variation in our movements. This time we have to march on, *to spread ourselves,* to stand, to march off. Before, the audience saw us in a dense mass: now, they will see us in scattered groups. No doubt there will be a great deal of talk afterwards, some people preferring us in a solid body, others delighting in the scattered effect, in which individual features, the fit of a black tight, for example, are brought into greater prominence.

Here is the second big scene—the wedding. All Verona is turning out. We see to it that our hats are not on straight, we grasp our pikes and

on we go, spreading ourselves superbly. The post
of honour falls to me. I am on guard at the church
door itself, actually between it and the footlights,
which are not two feet away. I am standing gracefully at ease. I am also wondering what would
happen if I dropped my pike, which now seems
about twenty feet long. Would it brain the *cor
anglais* player in the trench below? Very busy
they are too, down there. I can see them all quite
plainly. I can see rows of faces in the stalls and
the circle. All the people in the chorus are singing now, so I join in, finding Gounod well within
my powers. It is absurd perhaps that the pikeman
on duty should sing, but then it is equally absurd
that anybody else there should sing. The drama
moves. I have a strong desire to drop my pike
or alternatively to play a bigger part in the action. Why shouldn't a humble member of the
town guard—the one with the black tight—suddenly become the hero of *Romeo and Juliet?*
Again, why shouldn't we pikemen take charge
of the whole drama, beginning by clearing the
stage? That would be a welcome diversion. What
would happen if we passed a note on to the management saying that we would clear the stage
with our pikes unless we were given five pounds

apiece? After all, we hold the opera in the hollow of our hands. We also hold our pikes, and I for one am tired of mine. There, it is finished. At least, the real opera is finished—the pike part of it—for there is still a little for Romeo and Juliet and other minor characters to do. We return to the depths, pikes at the trail; we throw black and yellow tights and bobbed wigs at the little bored man; we wash and dress and receive our money; we depart for beer.

Such was my début in opera. This is exactly what happened, just ten years ago. I have invented nothing; I have neither exaggerated nor embellished; yet I do not expect to be believed.

S O FAR this summer seems to have been passed
in the shadow of Punch. There are four children in this house and they hardly ever think
about anything but Punch—not the paper but the
genuine puppet. He can be seen on the beach every
morning and afternoon, and as often as they are
allowed to, the children pay him a visit. They are
for ever talking about him, discussing him as you
or I might discuss Mr. Baldwin, though with more
excitement. And nearly every evening, between tea
and bedtime, they all act Punch. We seem to have
rented a house in Punchdom. If I were to walk
out one of these evenings and discover that the
beach and promenade were crowded with Punches,
Judies, babies, clowns, policemen, beadles, hangmen, comic boxers, and crocodiles, I should not
be very surprised. The real people here are quite
shadowy. The place is completely dominated by
these antique but energetic puppets. I have never
seen the mayor of the town, but if I did see him
and found that he had a tremendous red nose,
staring eyes, a cocked hat and a hump, I doubt

if I should be startled. If the town clerk wears a frill in place of a collar, has red spots on his face, and calls himself Joey, I shall refuse to be astonished. Why, even the fishermen here have suspiciously squeaky voices, and there is something curiously wooden about them. And those men who call out as one passes, 'Obble-obble-obble on the motor-boat, sir,' or something like that, is there not something queer about them?

The children, who had not met Mr. Punch before, fell at once, victims of his conquering cudgel. Last year's pantomime could not compare with him. To tell the truth, they hardly laughed at all at the pantomime. Astonishingly nimble and industrious drolls tumbled about the stage, smashed crockery, threw flour and water at one another, but all to no purpose. The children regarded them with wide innocent eyes, into which there crept, after a time, a certain hardening of contempt. I laughed until the tears ran down my cheeks, especially at the man who, being told to count the cups and plates, promptly smashed them with a hammer, but the children hardly smiled. The eldest of them was simply indignant with the plate-smashing man; she said he was 'stupid'; she knew that that was no way to count plates.

No, the pantomime was not a success. But the moment they saw Mr. Punch, they were enraptured. His performance was not a large and confusing affair, like the pantomime; it was small and delightful and, in its own fantastic way, sensible. I doubt if they had ever been told anything about Punch, but they understood him at a glance and he immediately took a place beside Red Ridinghood and the Three Bears. Indeed, he soon became more important, if only because you had only to go down to the beach to find him doing something, and perhaps something he had never done before. In one bound he became the most important person in the place, one to be discussed from every point of view. There was great talk in the nursery about 'Mr. Punch's house,' and I was consulted almost at once, for I am regarded there as an authority on what are called 'funnies.' The general impression seems to be that Punch and I are old friends—probably at school together. I do my best to live up to this greatness that has been thrust upon me, but it is very hard work.

Punches differ, I suppose. We are lucky in ours here. He is a Punch of temperament. Thus, he will not come out at all until the younger members of the audience have shouted—and at the

very top of their voices too—that they are ready
and waiting. 'Louder, louder!' he squeaks from
the mysterious depths; and all the children yell
away. But once he is out, you could not ask for
a more free-and-easy fellow. He is not one of your
Punches who must go through the routine adventures with babies and hangmen and will not do
anything else. No, our Punch likes to have fun
with everybody. He is mischievous and he is also
very conceited—'That's the way to do it,' he is
always saying, like the artist he is—but he is the
best playfellow in the world. His gusto is magnificent. He does not merely throw the baby out
once, he throws it out any number of times. No
sooner has it gone than he asks to have it back
so that he can throw it out again. His fun with
the Master is endless. (The Master is the man who
stands at the side—when he is not going round
with the hat.) He even steals the Master's hat and
throws a frying pan at him. He is fond of luring
little boys to stand close to the stage, and then he
likes to snatch their caps. If little girls come up,
he insists upon kissing them—'Kissee, kissee,
kissee,' he squeaks shamelessly—and he always
tells the Master that he wants to kiss all the
bigger girls, who are standing at the back. This

« 19 »

he is not allowed to do, so frequently he encourages a bout between two unusually ferocious boxers, who fight so long that both are tired out and are then knocked on the head very easily. At other times, he will give out prizes or sing songs that the children must repeat after him. How they shout when he asks them, as he always does, if they have seen the baby or the crocodile!

Some time ago there arrived at this house a large parcel, out of which came a Punch, a Judy with a particularly long, unpleasant face, a Baby that looked like a member of a German Youth movement, a beadle or other functionary with a three-cornered hat, a policeman with a red beard and a spiked helmet—a creature too exotic for our taste, and a Devil, horns and all. This was the best that the toy-shop (and Germany) could do for us in the matter of children's Punch sets, and though there was no clown (a great loss), no crocodile, and no hangman, we managed very well. These puppets had not been with us a week, however, before Mr. Punch, this new little Mr. Punch, of course, not the real one on the beach, was lost. Search parties went out, but he was never found. He may have gone back to Germany; he may have run away with another and prettier

Judy; he may have been frightened by the bigger Punch; we do not know what happened to him. Out of this catastrophe, however, I plucked the white flower of one ecstatic afternoon, during which I turned the Devil into Punch. I cut off his horns; I carved the face; I scraped off what was left of the old paint; then with a sixpenny box of colours from Woolworth's I repainted the face, made a fine hat out of the corner of a stout foolscap envelope, and—behold!—the Devil was no more and Punch had come back again. Is there an allegory in this?

And now my Punch gives a show, popping up from behind an armchair or settee and speaking, 'That's the way to do it', at least once a day here. He throws things nearly as well as the proper Punch down on the beach. Indeed, he is rather too enthusiastic about throwing things. But a wonderful thing has happened—to him, to all of us. This needs the glory of italics and it shall have them. *He has been recognized by the proper Mr. Punch.* Isn't that amazing? But that is not all. Not only has our little Punch been recognized by his big brother, but so have all the four children. It happened one morning last week, and we were so excited afterwards that we could hardly eat our lunch. Somebody in this house must have guessed that something unusual was about to happen because the children were told that they could go and see Punch and take their own puppet with them—but that only makes it all the more mysterious. Mr. Punch called up all the four children; he knew their names; he knew that one of them had been ill not long ago; and he knew that they had a little Punch of their own, and when he saw him, he was very pleased and proud, so that you could tell at once that our Punch really was a member of the family.

If you should point out that we are overdoing this Punch business, I doubt if I should disagree with you. There can be too much Punchery. You are beginning to think that we are snobs, with our 'Punch this' and 'Punch that.' I suppose we are. But—dash it all!—do you realize that we know him, that he has spoken to us? Has he ever spoken to you? No, I thought not.

THE DISILLUSIONED

I T WAS our experience at the circus last Tuesday afternoon that compelled me to reflect upon this matter. Even the children were disappointed when we actually visited that circus. For weeks we had been staring at the coloured bills, across which was pasted the startling slip: *For One Day Only*. There was a most artful crescendo of this bill-posting. Every day the children announced that they had seen new pictures of the circus and thereupon reported fresh wonders. Elephants and tigers and ponies and clowns and cowboys, all superb in the three-colour process, claimed more and more space on our hoardings, from which auctioneers and estate agents and other dull fellows were banished. Nero and Heliogabalus themselves, if they had caught a glimpse of our hoardings, would have decided to stay on in the town.

Now I do not say that it was a bad little travelling circus, but I do say that it was certainly not the circus of the coloured bills. There were no lions and tigers at all. Instead of a whole crazy regiment of clowns, there were only two, and they were rather dingy fellows. The cowboys turned out to be the men who had first shown us to our seats, and though their hats and boots undoubtedly came from the Wild West, between these extremities all three of them were too homely for our taste. Where was the long procession of elephants, each of them as big as a house? There were only two elephants and they seemed quite small after those monsters of the hoardings. 'I think they must be young elephants,' said one of the children. 'They're awfully small, aren't they?'

I do not say that our visit was a failure. (The two younger children have been circus ponies ever since and do nothing but trot round in circles.) But I do think it would have been a far greater success if we had never seen all those lying pictures. Our hopes were raised too high, so that disappointment was inevitable. The children naturally assumed they would see in reality all that the poster artists and the printers had contrived for them. They are still puzzled about it. They invent excuses for the proprietor. The other elephants must have gone for a walk or run after the missing lions and tigers. Forty clowns or so—and those that have the nicest costumes too—must not have been feeling very well. It is almost pathetic to hear them thus excusing the cunning old fabulist. These children are growing up in a world of artful advertisement. Only the other day, one of them, who can read quite nicely, chanced to read an advertisement of some domestic commodity and cried: 'Mummie, it says it's the *best* in all the world. Why don't you *buy* some?' Here was this precious stuff, the best in the world, to be had for the asking, and we were stupidly doing nothing about it. Soon she will realize that the matter was not quite so urgent as she imagined. Even now she may be thinking in secret that perhaps the man who owned the circus and put out all those false pictures of it had simply taken her in. Disillusion is already dogging her footsteps.

This is, I understand, an age of disillusion. It is also an age in which the business of suggesting that many things are perfect has become a highly organized trade or profession. I suspect that there is some connexion between these two facts. Consider our position. Men have always dreamed of perfection, but in past ages they did not think of perfection as existing at all in the ordinary world. It was always somewhere round the corner. If you could find your way into the Garden of the Hesperides, to the Isles of the Blest, to that secret Avalon where there was neither rain nor snow, then there you would come upon life made perfect. If you were a poet, a dreamer, an idealist, you found a quiet corner and thought about these beautiful places. If your wine was sourer than usual and your new tunic was shredding away, you shrugged your shoulders, then remembered that in the Hesperides or Avalon all the wine was unimaginably delicious and tunics lasted just as long as you wanted them to last. I do not doubt for a moment that in those days merchants concocted their fables and hucksters cried up their wares most monstrously. But there was certainly no elaborate machinery for pointing out that all manner of things were perfect. The whole world was not told to Drink Aristides' Wine And Never Have a Headache, that Trunk Hose From Richard Whittington's Wear For Ever. There was no large-scale attempt to introduce the Philosopher's Stone or the Fountain of Youth into every home. It was not generally understood that the payment of a first instalment or even the filling in of a coupon would anchor the Isles of the Blest outside your front door.

Nowadays we do not believe that life that is all goodness, truth, and beauty is being lived somewhere beyond the nearest mountains or the western seas. All the enchanted islands have vanished. We have even stopped singing about Dixie, which I take to be one—and apparently the last —of these ideal realms. But have we suddenly forgotten how to dream of perfection? I think not. There is no perfect life going on round the corner, but now, surely, it is even nearer than that. In front of me, at this moment, are two magazines, one English and the other American, the kind with shiny paper and expensive advertisements; and in the pages at the beginning and end of these magazines I find reports of life that has been made perfect.

I do not know where to begin. When I turn over these pages I am bewildered, mazed with good news. Reflect upon the irritations, the boredoms, the long grinding tragedies, of this life of ours. Be brave for a moment and remember the dismal antics of our bodies; our fatty tissues and acids in the stomach, our gout and dyspepsia and startling blood pressures, our failing sight and thinning hair and rotting teeth. Keep steadily in mind the days when you have not been able to entertain yourself and the nights when you have not been able even to entertain your friends. Think how

« 27 »

we suffer from clothes that do not fit, boots that wear out, raincoats that drink like sponges, tobacco that burns the tongue, whisky that is new and raw, cars that will not take hills in top-gear, mattresses that do nothing but sag, and trains that are always late. All these, from the huge miseries that come crashing into our lives like a rhinoceros to the little irritations that bite like mosquitos, have disappeared. The people here know nothing about them. They are as gods. Look at the women —seven foot tall, beautifully slender, exquisitely gowned and hatted, their hair so cunningly and crisply waved! Look at the men—so ruddy of cheek and bright of eye, so broad and square in the shoulders, so astonishingly tailored and laundered! What domestic felicity they enjoy! 'Welcome home!' they cry, for ever smiling and holding out their arms.

Examine the children—they are called 'Kiddies' here—and notice their apple-cheeks, their sturdy limbs, their playfulness that never, never turns into naughtiness, into stamping and screaming. In winter they sit in front of bright fires (Coal, Gas, Electric) and listen happily to the World's Masterpieces of Music; they recline in chairs so marvellously sprung that they would never get up out of them if they did not know that upstairs were the most comfortable mattresses ever offered to the public and instant sleep induced by a cup of Whatisit. In summer they sprawl on gamboge sands by the side of a royal blue sea, in perpetual sunshine, and have to hand pipes that will not crack, the aristocrat of cigarettes, bottles of elixir (various brands); and the men look more god-like than ever, partly because their hair has been fixed for the day by a little cream; the women, fully protected against sun-burn, are dazzlingly beautiful and gracious; and the kiddies, well stuffed with a miraculous breakfast food, are growing an inch a day—and all their clothes are growing with them. (Even the suitcases are quietly expanding in the box-room.) And winter or summer, their watches never go wrong and their shoes never pinch; they never worry or mope or quarrel; they never sicken and die. And this, we are told, is not Avalon but our own world.

Alas! we are for ever discovering that it is not our own world, that try as we may—sending off at once, refusing all imitations, filling in coupons, paying first instalments—we cannot reproduce the life of these people in the advertisements. There is always a catch. We are always being taken in. There are only two clowns and two elephants. Thus, living in an age of advertisement, we are perpetually disillusioned. The perfect life is spread before us every day, but it changes and withers at a touch—never a Snark, always a Boojum.

CARLESS AT LAST

I SUPPOSE there are thousands of people in this country who are now telling themselves that they are happy because at last they have cars. But what is their happiness compared with mine? At odd moments throughout the day I remember that I have no car, and there is more music in my heart than ever came out of Daventry Experimental. Sometimes I forget that it has really gone for ever. I think of it being away in some garage, eating its head off; I imagine that I shall soon have to go once more and hear the lying reports of the mechanics; I take up my letters expecting to find among them those bills for repairs that are as crazy and vindictive as the proclamations of Oriental tyrants. And then I remember. It has gone for ever; there are no more garages, mechanics, bills for repair; I am no longer an owner-driver but a free man. There is an astonishing feeling of lightness and ease about the shoulders. No longer have I to support a huge and dubious piece of mechanism and its sneering and shrugging attendants in overalls. The thing may have made me look richer than I am, but it certainly made me feel miserably poor. Now that it has gone, I seem to be quite comfortably off again. I take trains and buses and taxis (without having to ask myself 'Why don't you use the car?') and I am amazed to find how cheap they are. It is a pleasure to travel now. It is also a pleasure to stay at home, for now there is no five-seater open tourer on the premises to remind me that I ought to be going somewhere in it in order to get my money's worth.

My mind to me a kingdom is. The R.A.C. and the A.A. are fading into meaningless initials. Double Shell is something in an ugly dream. I pass Dunlop and Michelin without so much as a nod. The Golden Pump is one of the innumerable blots on the landscape, nothing more. If any more young men don overalls and dirty their faces, they will not do it at my expense. I am indifferent to the real character of Ethyl. Four, six, eight, or twenty cylinders, it is all one to me now. What they do to the gallon is a question that leaves me shrugging, and at last I have enough spare cash to discover, if necessary, what I can do to the gallon. I can look at the country-side again like a man and not like a mere slave of the wheel. I can afford to dislike your long straight roads, to

« 32 »

welcome the narrowest and most winding of lanes.
I like to see trams in a town. The sight of cattle
in the streets give me pleasure again. I smile at
old ladies who wander into the middle of the
road and then decide to turn back. The cyclist
seems to me an innocent creature, not without a
certain quaint beauty. I have shed a whole foul
tangle of contempt and envy. The people who sit
in long shining pieces of mechanism no longer
seem any better than the people who are packed
into a tiny box on wheels. I raise no more hats
to the Rolls or the Daimler: neither do I put out
my tongue at the oldest Ford. In that daft world
of wheels and smells I am Gallio himself. I am
happy and free, careless and carless. It is as if my
mind—the metaphor comes to me from some
vague dream—had been decarbonized.

I was never at ease in that world. True, the
first car I had was an unusually incompetent, if
not downright malicious, vehicle. It was a very
good argument for mass production, for it was
of a make so rare that I never found anybody
who had ever heard of it, and most people seemed
to imagine that I had invented the name—and
probably made the car. There was always one part
of the mechanism that was not working, and to-

wards the end hardly anything was working; I remember taking one visitor to the station in it when neither footbrake nor handbrake, clutch nor gears, were doing duty, and even the steering-wheel was all loose—we simply rolled down to the station. The only advantage the car had over ordinary cars was that it required virtually no feeding. I never remember giving it any oil, and it only asked for a mere drop of petrol. I suspect that it was not an internal-combustion engine at all, but a car on a new principle—years before its time—and really worked by will-power. Probably in a century or two there will be nothing but cars like that, which will simply be *thought* along the road. Unfortunately, my own will was not strong enough, though undoubtedly I worked miracles with it. Men in garages regarded me with wonder and awe after they had examined it, and I have no doubt the more intolerant of these mechanics would have had me burned as a wizard if I had stayed in the neighbourhood.

My second—and last—car was very different. It was the product of a very well known firm, and it looked imposing enough. It worked in the ordinary way, and so long as various expensive operations were performed upon it from time to time, it continued to work. But instead of being an ascetic, it was a downright glutton. Petrol it consumed as fast as it could, but oil was its passion. It demanded the most extravagant brands, and it could never have enough of them. It would hardly visit the station under a quart, and when we went touring in it you could have followed our route simply by observing the trail of empty oil drums. I could never afford to buy myself a book or a cigar or a bottle of wine when I had that car, for as soon as I had a spare pound or two it cried out for more oil. It was like entertaining for ever a drunkard who touched nothing but champagne. Imagine the relief at seeing him reel away at last, and you can form an idea of my present state of mind. I cannot pass a garage without jingling the shillings in my pocket and feeling comparatively rich.

That I am a bad driver I will cheerfully admit. I think the trouble about driving is that it requires just the wrong amount of attention—at least from me. It is not absolutely a full-time job, needing all your concentrated powers, but neither is it a thing you can do properly while thinking about something else. This was always my mistake: I would go on so merrily that after a time

I would begin to think about other things, and when I did return to the matter in hand I was always a few seconds too late. I was too late at High Wycombe, when I bent the front axle; at Ealing when I hit the tram; at Northwood when I ran into the oldest Ford in the world (it belonged to a bill-poster and smashed my radiator); at Newport, that horrible November afternoon, when I cracked the electric standard and gathered round me all the people of Monmouth. When I was not too dreamy I was too impatient. Thick traffic exasperated me. My friend P. actually likes driving through thick traffic, and spends many a happy hour reversing in the most crowded London thoroughfares. Such a taste is incomprehensible to me. It is as if a man liked putting in a morning doing up the most awkwardly shaped objects into parcels, at the risk of being fined or maimed if they were not absolutely neat. My own experiences were so unpleasant that merely to be a passenger in a car that is being driven through a tangle of traffic makes me sweat; and in Paris I shut my eyes and offer up a prayer. It is not that I am afraid of being killed or of killing anybody else (I was never in danger of doing that even when I drove myself); it is simply the thought of that familiar and sickening crash, the crowd and the questions and the fuss, that appals me, remembering as I do my own adventures.

Now I am well out of it, a free man again. I suffer no inconvenience, for there is no longer any pleasure in motoring itself and there are trains and buses and taxis enough to take me wherever I want to go. No more taxes and garage fees and bills for petrol and oil. No more maddening conferences with mechanics who know no more about cars than I do, and no more staggering charges for repairs. No more worries about good roads and bad roads and trams and policemen. I can no longer drop you anywhere. You will have to drop me, and when I go, notice how jaunty my step, how lively the tune I whistle, all so carless and free.

THE SKIPPER

I HAVE seen a contented man. He was the skipper of the tiny steamer that took us up the Meuse. I do not know that officially he was in charge of the boat, which had the air of being the only little bit of perfect democracy on this earth. I never heard anybody giving orders. There were only three in the crew. I do not count the man who gave us tickets (he had a long sallow face and steel spectacles, and he reminded me vaguely of the illustrations in the American funny books I used to read when I was a boy, Max Adeler's *Elbow Room* and the like) and the vast dripping head that emerged from the engine-room as members of the crew. Two of these were nondescript young men, merely elastic-sided boots and peaked caps. They too were contented, but that was simply because they had achieved peaked caps. A Belgian of the humbler classes asks no more from life than to be allowed to wear a peaked cap. He aims at that just as a member of the middle classes there aims at a long and astonishingly unreal beard and a new leather portfolio. Our man, the skipper, was older, and it was he who took the wheel for the greater part of the journey, though he was not above surrendering it and taking his turn at hopping off and tying up the boat. He was one of those short thick-set grizzled men with very deep voices that are so familiar in France and Belgium. You might describe him as a curly Old Bill. He wore a short coat, made of some thin black material like alpaca, and a pair of trousers so baggy, so voluminous in the seat, that he could have turned round inside them. It is not easy to be dignified in such trousers, and a peaked cap too small for you and elastic-sided boots will not make the task any easier. But he was dignified.

When I first stepped on to the steamer at Namur and met his eye, I knew at once that we were all in his charge. It was inevitable that he should take the wheel. He sat there, still smoking his clay pipe, nonchalantly enough, and as he spun the wheel and stared ahead with little deepset eyes, he looked like something between a sailor and an engine-driver—a happy compromise. Whatever the Meuse had in store for us, no matter what currents and reefs and shoals were waiting above, he would see us safely through. Even if the German guns roared again over the hills, he

« 39 »

would still see us safely through. He tugged at a cord and the steamer told all Namur that we were off. The other four elastic-sided boots hopped ashore; the ropes were untied; the boots hopped back; and off we went. For the first ten minutes or so all was easy. We had the whole sparkling breadth of the river to sail in, and our skipper never took his pipe out of his mouth. But then I saw him put his pipe down. I looked ahead, and there noticed a kind of weir and a lock for our steamer, a very narrow lock. There seemed only a few feet to spare at the entrance to it, but the skipper gave a spin this way and a spin that, and in we glided, so smoothly that the four elastic sides were able to hop out before we came to rest. As soon as she was tied up, the skipper descended from his wheel. Calmly he surveyed the lock. Calmly—though perhaps with a hint of derision —he spat into it. Then he turned again to his clay pipe.

At the next lock but one—a very ticklish fel-low—he produced a bottle and without haste or any loss of dignity he tilted it towards the blue spaces and the clouds that were sailing faster than we were. Having refreshed himself and lit his pipe again, he exchanged jests in the deepest bass with a mysterious personage in a peaked cap who always seemed to pop up at every lock. Perhaps it was not the same man every time, but it always looked like the same man. Then he took stock of us, his charges. The pair of lovers from Namur were photographing one another for the fifth time. The man with a straw hat, attached to himself, after the manner of the ancients, by a black cord, was relighting his cigar again. The two women with the baby boy were once more leading the baby boy carefully round the deck. The middle-aged woman with the pink hat was still reading Maurice Dekobra, from whom she had not yet lifted her eyes. The two men with forked beards were eating sandwiches; they had been eating sandwiches all along; I could not imagine them without sandwiches. I do not know what the skipper thought of us. Perhaps he thought we were not worth taking up the Meuse, guiding in and out of locks. But he gave no sign. He did not care about us, I think; he had his little steamer, answering its helm so beautifully; he had his fine clay pipe and convenient bottle and (as we discovered at the next lock but two) his lunch all snug in a round tin; he had his position at Namur and Dinant, and a welcome all the way between;

« 41 »

and I have no doubt that somewhere not too far from the water's edge he had a wife as sturdy as himself, some broad-faced children, and a pot of onion soup.

I thought I saw, written in the comfortable lines about his eyes, the conviction that river steamers are best of all. It was a conviction I shared with him that morning, when the river was all dancing light and the green hills of the Ardenne country softly unwound themselves about us. Only on a river steamer do you see the world glide past like a happy dream. There is indeed something dreamlike about the very motion of this journeying. Not one day in a hundred on the open sea brings you this sensation. There, you are always inside a thing that is driving hard against the water or being buffeted, and you alternate between epic poetry and the foulest and most ungovernable prose. A voyage down a river is like pleasant light verse. I except all your Amazons and Mississippis, yellow floods a mile or two wide. The river must be small, companionable.

All the way along I was reminded of something. Every corner we turned in the river tantalized me. I had certainly never been there before, yet I felt I knew it or something like it. We were nearly at the end of our voyage before I saw what it was. I was gliding towards the frontier of the fairy tale country. I have always felt that somewhere between France and Belgium and Germany is the country where the fairy tales happened. It must be somewhere near Luxemburg, yet I knew that it was not Luxemburg, for I had been there. Probably you can never approach this frontier in a train, and certainly not in one of those international wagonlit affairs. That would explain why I had never found the country of the fairy tales when I had been this way before. But a fellow might easily sneak into the place in one of these tiny river steamers, themselves like toys. Thus I argued, and everything I saw seemed to prove that we were not far away. The woods hanging above us were thicker and greener than ever, and were the very image of that wood where the Sleeping Beauty was hidden. I caught a glimpse of a château with curly towers, perched on the summit of a grey crag, and there was Marquis of Carabbas written all over it. And then I remembered the ginger-bread. At Namur I had noticed hundreds of little men and animals made of ginger-bread; at Dinant there had been more ginger-bread still, and its men and animals had been far larger; and

« 43 »

now, it seemed, we might arrive any moment at a place where the ginger-bread figures would be life-size, perhaps all bobbing and smiling at us along the river bank. I watched the skipper anxiously. Everything depended on him. An extra turn or two of the wheel and he might land us there.

But he didn't. Perhaps he thought we were not worthy. When the little ship was tied up for the last time and he came down from the wheel, I examined cautiously that rubicund front of his, shining now with the knowledge of duty done, still wearing its air of large contentment. For a second or so it seemed like a mask. Surely there was a curious glint in the eye, a wrinkle or two that had not been there before that hinted at mockery? I had finished my *potage du jour* before I had stopped wondering.

IN DEFENCE OF KINDNESS

'OH YES, you have plenty of ki-hindness now. . . . Oh yes, America's treacled the world over with ki-hindness. Daley's kind—democracy's always dreadfully kind. Kindness is a symptom of vulgarity.' This is said by one of Miss Benson's characters, apparently a crazy and embittered old woman, and we have no right to saddle the author herself with it. Probably these are not her sentiments. But I cannot help thinking that possibly they are. I admire Miss Benson's fiction and consider her perhaps the best of all the excess-of-self-consciousness school of young feminine novelists. I do not see her, however, as the perfectly detached creative artist, and there is in the passage quoted above a suspicious gusto. Moreover, I have read Miss Benson before, and seem to remember various remarks that indicated a not dissimilar attitude of mind. It is not an attitude of mind that I can easily understand. But then, I believe in kindness. Even when it is called 'ki-hindness,' I still believe in it. If America is full of kindness, if democracy is always dreadfully kind, so much the better for America and democracy. If kindness is a symptom of vulgarity, then let us be vulgar.

Nearly all our younger 'intellectual' novelists seem to share this strange attitude towards goodwill. They have a common delight in lonely aristocratic persons, selfish, violent, cruel, as sociable as wolves. Their god, Mr. D. H. Lawrence, perpetually creates characters that are like wild animals in rut. All Mr. Liam O'Flaherty's personages seem to be violent creatures who are for ever tightening their jaws, grinding their teeth, and meditating murder. Even Mr. Aldous Huxley, for all his intellectual high spirits, can only find room for cruel little puppets, and has given us Peacockian comedy robbed of its geniality. The women novelists are not so much in love with violence as the men, but they are no more in love with kindness, and if anything are more resolutely opposed to it. It is strange what a passion so many serious young female novelists have always had for selfish bullying males. 'Why,' asked Thackeray, years ago, 'why do our lady novelists make the men bully the women?' The question is still with us. And now there are others. Why are all these brilliant contemporaries of ours so strangely lost in admiration of ruthlessness? What is it that attracts them towards cruelty, physical or mental? Why do they take care to remove their heroes and heroines such a distance from anything like good-humour? Why does one touch of kindness make the whole world sin?

I can ask these questions, and a hundred more as tedious, but I must confess that I cannot answer them. I ought to be able to answer them. I am not peering wistfully at these writers through a fog of years: they are more or less of my own generation, and have grown up in the same world. But there are times when I wonder if they really have grown up in the same world. They write as if this earth had known a thousand years as easy as a feather bed, as if no angry word had been spoken within the memory of man, as if rage and violence and cruelty and ruthless self-seeking were only to be found in a few antique fables. They would seem to have had the same astonishing experience of human relations as Kingsley must have had of English weather when he welcomed his wild North-easter and cried:

> Tired we are of summer,
> Tired of gaudy glare,
> Showers soft and steaming,
> Hot and breathless air.

THE BALCONINNY

Tired of listless dreaming,
Through the lazy day. . . .

I can well imagine a band of ardent young
spirits protesting against a world grown soft with
kindness, declaring that the time had arrived when
these long centuries of ease in which not only
had there been no wars, feuds, crimes or violence,
but not even private quarrels and angry disputes,
nothing indeed but loving words and gentle
glances, must come to an end, or there would be
no spirit and passion left in the race of men. When
they glanced through their newspapers and discovered that employers in England were insisting
on raising their men's wages, and the men were
determined to work longer hours, that members
of the Russian Government had said 'Dear, dear!'
to a gentleman who had been publicly advocating
a political change, that a large crowd in Georgia
had recently wept over an erring negro, I can
imagine them talking wistfully of the strenuous
old days. Not being of an ardent or reforming
temper, I shrink from joining movements, but
in these circumstances, even I would be disposed
to join the band of protestants, and might go
the length of working up a little quarrel in print

« 48 »

with a fellow author, probably the first that would have happened for several generations.

The world I have known, however, has been so different that I am removed as yet by whole ages from accepting any such point of view. If America has treacled the world over with kindness, then all I can say is that my footsteps have been singularly free from all traces of this syrup. Indeed, so fantastic has been my experience that I cling to the belief that our world is not suffering from an excess of good feeling but from a lack of it. I am one of those who have lagged so far behind that they still see kindness as an ideal in human relations, and have not yet made the discovery that human happiness is menaced by it. They try hard to be kind to other people, and even if they met Miss Benson's poisonous old lady they would try to be kind to her. So, too, they are anxious that other people should be kind to them. Only a lunatic, a monster of pride, could possibly be infuriated by other people's kindness. It is, I admit, extremely annoying to be the victim of people's pretended kindness, but that is because you are being offered a counterfeit of something really precious. The thought of a world in which kindness predominates does not make most of us angry, it makes us wistful, for in such a world we should be able to do all manner of things that we cannot do now: for example, we should be able to spend more time reading the works of our younger and brilliant novelists, whose lonely and ruthless aristocratic personages might then prove to be better company than they are at present. As it is, I for one cannot share their creators' admiration for them.

I cannot help suspecting that behind much of this delight in violence, ruthlessness, trampling egoism, there are some little tragi-comedies of weak nerves, frustration, and injured vanity. Many of these writers, notwithstanding their excellence as literary craftsmen, have not yet escaped the childish desire—as people say—to get their own back. This is perhaps surprising in authors whose powers suggest maturity, if only because it is usually associated with immaturity. I remember that when I was a publisher's reader, going through piles of manuscripts, mostly novels, every week, I was always coming across attempts at fiction that were nothing but infantile day-dreams. In these the hero or heroine was frequently very rude to everybody, and went tearing through life like a battle-cruiser. These novels, I am convinced, were always the work of timid governesses and shy little clerks in lodgings, who were heartily sick of being over-looked and snubbed, perhaps angry because they found it impossible to assert themselves, and so every night they turned happily to their foolscap and a dream-life in which they were strong, tower-ing, ruthless. And given the intensity and verbal force, literature can be made out of such day-dreaming, even when it is nothing but the desire to get one's own back, a childish beating with the fists on the locked door of life. But not, I think, the best kind of literature. It is significant that all the great virile writers, who have grappled closely with life, detest nothing so much as this hardness, pride, egoism. Thus, it was out of this material that Shakespeare manufactured his villains and butts, who are rapidly becoming our heroes, for you will find Iago and Malvolio stalking triumphantly through a good many of our modern novels and plays. Shakespeare would have turned that old woman who so disliked 'ki-hindness' into a witch. When he and his fellows in the art want to praise anything in this life, it is precisely kindness that they praise, not realizing perhaps that the time would come, immediately after the halcyon years of the Great War, when the world would be suffering from a surfeit of gentle looks and loving speech.

I WISH you would,' said the tiny voice in the telephone. 'Look here, could you come at once? I'll send the car up for you. It'll be much quicker.' And then he rang off, like the rich and masterful fellow he is. Within twenty minutes a long crimson car was at my door. I descended and found the chauffeur waiting there, very dapper in his blue uniform. He saluted when I approached, then held open the door of the saloon for me. For about half a minute I felt rather rich and masterful myself. That is the advantage of being a member of the middle classes; you know all kinds of people, plutocrats to paupers, and can contrive to enjoy all kinds of sensations, from the opulencies of the rich to the stinging ironies of the poor.

When I had settled into a corner, the chauffeur handed me a rug, heavy with fur, and I wrapped this luxurious thing round my legs. I was now at ease in what was virtually a little crimson sitting-room. True, it was cold and smelled of leather, but nevertheless it was a room.

The chauffeur had now closed the door on me and seated himself in front. My room began to move down the street. I leaned back and closed my eyes, confident that this little room would be guided half-way across London until at last it reached its owner. But no sooner had I cosily come to terms with this confidence than I began to question it. What right had I to assume so easily that I should reach my destination? Every day the papers are filled with the names of people who imagined they would reach their destinations and did not. 'We'll just slip round in the car to Uncle Harry's,' they told one another. But there was no Uncle Harry for them—only an agonizing twist or two, a few screams, then darkness, an Arctic night, death.

I opened my eyes again and saw the runaway length of Fitzjohn's Avenue, which looked as if it intended to shoot us like a bullet into the tangle of traffic down there at Swiss Cottage. Its villas whizzed backward and upward, past the windows of my little room. An elderly man stood in front of us, hesitating. Perhaps his pockets were full of sweets for his grandchildren, and he was thinking about them. The car did not scream, jeer or hoot at him, as some cars do: it quietly rapped out

'Murder, murder!' He drew back, just in time, and we slip past him. It was then that I began to consider the chauffeur. All that I could see of him directly was a blue back and a uniform cap, a little to one side. I could catch glimpses, however, of his reflected face in the glass in front. I could see his pale eyes, which had a curious little slant to them. Indeed, though his colouring was European enough, there was something Mongolian about his features. A broad flat face and a slant to the eye. I did not know his name or anything about him, and here I was, sitting behind him, dependent on every movement of his feet and turn of his wrist. He seemed steady enough, but suppose some little clot of blood was already out of its place, somewhere under that cap, and even now was about to transform all his ordered world of chauffeurdom into a dark screaming lunacy—what then? What became of me and my little room?

Swiss Cottage went past, and Maida Vale followed, and then we shot into gloomy little streets without a name. Lorries came thundering out of side-turnings, taxis waltzed impudently in front of us, pedestrians ran forward or dithered desperately in the middle of the road, other cars slid to right and left—and all on a greasy surface, the very treachery of winter. A sudden faint gleam showed that we had arrived in the neighbourhood of that canal which wanders about a little to the north of Paddington. Is it the Grand Junction Canal or the Regent's Canal? I do not know, and the canal itself does not look as if anyone else does either. I never saw a fouler length of water. It belongs not to commerce but to the London of a child's nightmare. If you read *Oliver Twist* a few years before you ought to, things like that canal come creeping into the panorama of the night. It is there to tempt little drudges from the basements of boarding-houses and maddened and half-witted lads to suicide. Somewhere, perhaps not very far away, in the stony wilderness of North-West London, that canal quietly joins the Styx.

A turn brought us alongside of the canal. Only a yard or two of ground and a miserable little wall separated us from the very water's edge. I looked through the window on my left, saw the faint leaden gleam, and shivered. Only a few yards away! And the road was slippery and steeply crowned. And we were travelling fast and the

car was very big and heavy. Suppose ——! I
looked out in front, and saw a lorry coming towards us, keeping far too near the middle of the
road and moving at a speed that no lorry should
attempt. Moreover, there was a man, a vague figure,
coming towards us too, and on our own side of
the road. And we rushed on, as if the road and
the canal were mere figments of a dream and our
very bones were immortal. Suppose ——! And
then it happened.

It all happened quite slowly, that is, there was
ample time for every conceivable thought, impulse,
sensation, though no time for any possible action
on my part. It is only tired novelists, bored with
their narrative, who try to make us believe that
things like this happen so quickly that we cannot
understand them. The mind, too, has its slow-
motion apparatus, and at the slightest signal from
Hell it begins working. When the huge trench-
mortar plomped into the very entrance of the little dug-out I was in at Souchez and then burst
the universe and left me for a while in primeval
dark and silence, there was time, even during the
seconds between its last express-train roar and the
explosion itself, to think and feel many things, and

perhaps I am still thinking and feeling them. There is time enough, after the tiger has made its spring, to tell yourself that the smell of its hot and bloody breath is indeed curious, unique. No, I shall not pretend that it happened so quickly that I cannot describe the event.

When the lorry was only a few yards away, a small car that had been masked by it shot forward from the back. The driver had evidently not seen us. It was bad enough that he should come out at all, but the next moment it was worse, for his car skidded when we were almost upon it. We were travelling at such a speed that there was no time for brakes, and my chauffeur desperately swung round his wheel. We gave a sickening turn. There was a shout. The man who was walking towards us, on our own side of the road, was there, and it looked as if he would be under our wheels in another second. Seeing him, the chauffeur must have swung round the wheel again, to the full limit of the lock. I know that I was flung down on the seat and ferociously bumped. For one scrambling second I saw nothing but plain sky out of the window. Then came the most awful crash. We had hit the wall. The wall had gone.

Some muddy ground rushed up at the nearest window and the whole car seemed to go heaving. Splash! and I was hurled forward against the partition. Splash!—we were in the canal. I had time to clutch a handle, but it was not the handle I wanted, and by the time I had found that, it was too late, the door could not be opened. Everything roared. Something was chiselling away at the top of my head. The water was in. It was all over us. Cold darkness rushed down on me, but inside my head huge rockets were bursting. There were shouts from somewhere, but they were far, far away, probably in another world.

I will not describe how the car was finally dragged out of the canal and our two dead bodies taken out of it. My imagination did not take me so far. I switched it off after we found Doomsday waiting for us in the canal. By this time we had passed the lorry and the pedestrian coming towards us, had left the canal behind and were travelling smoothly through that vague district known as Westbourne Park. I do not admit, however, that nothing had happened. I have described as accurately as I can what happened, and the event, you may be sure, has been entered into some queer archives somewhere in the universe. It had not the influential backing of Time and Space, and so I was able to reach my destination. The tiger did not spring, and so I am still alive. But I caught the gleam of an eye, a whiff of hot, rank breath. He was there all the time.

LITTLE TICH

O F ALL the deaths that occurred last year—
and how rich it was in mortuary—the one
that troubled my imagination most was that of
Little Tich. Hardy, Haig, Asquith, these are a
nation's losses; we bared our heads in the streets
or went black-plumed to the Abbey; our very
mourning was large, cool, and dignified, a state
pageant. The poet, the soldier, the statesman, these
have had their being in a world where death kept
his throne, and to go to the grave is for them
only the inevitable last journey. No sooner have
they gone than we fall to estimating and praising,
making new entries in the ledgers of fame; but
unless we stood close to these great departed, knew
them and loved them as men, we do not find ourselves staring anew at this life, bewildered by mortality. But it is inconceivable that a famous droll
should ever leave us. We cannot believe that he
and Death could ever meet. To go from the Al-
hambra to the grave—there is nothing inevitable
in this, but something bewildering, shocking. That
is why Hamlet, questioning this life, brooding

over mortality in the graveyard of Elsinore, finds
the skull of Yorick in his hand. Therefore I make
no apology for saying that none of these deaths
we have had lately has troubled me more than
that of Little Tich.

It has been said that the passing of these men
has brought an age to an end. Thus, with Hardy,
goes the last flicker of the Victorian Age of Literature. Nearly as much might be said of Little Tich,
whose very name takes us back to the distant idiocy
of the Tichborne Case. He was a legend in his
later years. He was capering in his long boots
when some of us, myself included, were in the
nursery. I heard about him—from uncles who
did not disdain to share the good news of life—
long before I ever set foot in a music hall. He was
one of the figures of the 'nineties. He had set in a
roar whole audiences of quaint extinct creatures,
'boys' with their bowler hats, yellow canes, and
short, pearl-buttoned, fawn coats, and 'girls' with
flounces and feather boas and dashing busts. Indeed, to the last, one of his songs used to bring
him on in the character of a 'masher', with short
fawn coat and tiny cane, one Johnny Green, or,
as he himself gave it out in the chorus, 'Ja-horny
Green, Ja-horny Green.' He came to us, unspoilt,

from the great days of the halls. He was a piece of social history. Something has departed with him, too. While we could still go and see him of an evening, we were in touch with another age. Now, the link has been broken.

These, however, are minor pedantries. I saw Little Tich many times, but never went with any thought of social history or past ages in my head. I can well remember the first time I saw him. I had heard so much that I had come, with all the cool arrogance of youth, to the conclusion that I should be disappointed. I suspected the hocus-pocus of memory working in my elders. The chap would probably be some mere freak, who made a name in drollery when such names were easy to make. The lights at the side flashed out the number of his turn; the band played very quickly and loudly; up went the curtain and there—in the middle of the enormous gold cavern of the stage—was a diminutive steeple-jack, complete with climbing apparatus. But he was no steeple-jack of this world; he had climbed into it from some other and infinitely droller world. There was something irresistibly comic in the foreshort-ened figure he presented. The head was of normal size, quite large as to nose; the body was trumpery; the legs were nothing, mere wisps. At once this astounding elf plunged into an account, illustrated by a wealth of passionate gestures, of the whole business of steeple-jackery; he seemed to climb, to tremble upon heights, to fall through space, before our very eyes; and there was in this manikin the fiery energy, the spirit, of ten men. In two minutes everybody was laughing. In five minutes I was laughing until the tears rolled down my cheeks. And many an hour have I laughed since, though never perhaps with that complete abandon of the first encounter. After I had seen him a few times, he did not make me laugh so much as keep me in a constant happy chuckling.

It was his habit to present a number of characters, a lady in court dress (perhaps his favourite), a grocer, a jockey, 'one of the boys,' and so on; and it was impossible not to be tickled by such a series of daft miniatures. You may say he drolly foreshortened all humanity. This trick helped, but it was not the secret of his attraction. Nor was it to be found in the obvious material of his turn. Thus his songs mattered not at all. You hardly ever caught the words of them, and when you did you found you had been listening to no purpose. The matter of his songs and talk was the old

traditional stuff—mother-in-law, the lodger, kip-
pers and beer, dubious sausages and dangerous
cheese; an ancient round of japes. But all this was
mere fodder for the unsophisticated, bait for the
groundlings. On a far higher level were his actions,
his sudden gestures.

The actions by means of which he illustrated
his little chronicles of triumph or woe were adorable. Indeed, they did not illustrate his tales, they
brought them to life. He would say, 'So I went
in,' and then he would show you how he went
in, his feet going pitter-patter-pitter-patter and his
tiny legs seeming to vibrate rather than move as
ordinary legs move. It was the essence of all going
in that he proffered you. He was magnificent when
he suggested a righteous indignation. Beginning
with some such remark as 'I told him what I
thought about him,' he would then proceed to
show you his disapproval in rich dumb-show, and
as he careered fiercely about the stage, kicking and
lungeing, the empty air was filled with retreating
giants. He had a trick of becoming entangled with
things—the train of that court dress, for example
—that few mimes in the world can have bettered;
and I will swear that his mounting fury, the old
anger of the human spirit baffled by stubborn

things, has never been surpassed. And his gestures, so quick and neat, so energetic and intelligent, were like little epigrams in a new language. No wonder he was so popular in Paris, where he numbered among his most enthusiastic admirers the Guitrys themselves. Now I come to think of it, there was something Gallic about this fiery little man. At times he would cock a knowing droll eye, taking a whole vast assembly into his confidence in a second, that said as much as two hours of French farce. But he was English too, cheerfully inconsequential. We talk of people 'breaking into' a dance, but the verb flatters them. Little Tich, however, really did break into dances. He was into a dance, fifty fantastic little steps, and out of it again almost before you knew what was happening.

There was in him an admirable sophistication in music-hall funny business. He really stood away from his songs and jokes and silly clothes and obvious fooling, and all the time merely offered them with a wink and a grin. The drollery was not in his doing these things but in his pretending to do them. He did not really act a man telling you something about his mother-in-law, but a man pretending to be a man telling you something

funny about his mother-in-law. You were all behind the scenes with him, or at least one set of
scenes, for behind another was a little hard-work-
ing actor called Relph, with a stout sense of his
dignity and importance in the profession and a
taste for painting. Thus he would offer a joke and
then shake his head over its reception, remarking
that it 'went better last night.' He would drop
his hat and then not be able to pick it up because
he always contrived to kick it forward. This might
or might not make you laugh. But when, having
done this a few times, he would say blandly:
'Comic business with chapeau,' then, if you shared
with him a free human intelligence, you shouted
with laughter. I think that was the innermost
secret of this little droll's appeal. In the antics
of this gargoyle there was all the time a suggestion of a companion spirit winking and nodding
and shrugging at you over the crazy jumble and
tangle of things. And the things remain, but he
has gone. Let us remember him with affection.

LECTURES

THERE is only one thing more foolish than going to hear a lecture and that, of course, is giving a lecture. I have suddenly realized that I have to give two lectures in the immediate future, and now I am telling myself that I am an ass to have undertaken these idiocies. As a rule, I am sensible enough about lectures. I never go to lectures and usually I refuse to give one. The Secretary of the Stocklington Literary Society assures me in vain that I am certain of a hearty welcome there any Tuesday in February. The fact that two of my books have been in (and out of, too) the Puddlefield Free Library does not tempt me to address the Puddlefield Institute any Friday in December.

I do not wish to give the impression that I am greatly in demand as a lecturer, because I am not, but I have enough sense to make sure that the demand is far greater than the supply. But now and again I am the victim of some maggot in the brain and cheerfully agree to visit some distant city and there make a fool of myself for about an hour.

Why I should ever do it, I do not know. There is no glory in it, no fun in it, as everybody knows. There is no money in it. The men who go round with lantern slides and bright talks on *Awheel in Albania* or *Forty Years a Hangman* may make a good thing out of it, but for us scribblers lecturing is a dead loss. And may I point out that all secretaries of literary societies overlook the fact that a writer must think economically in terms of time? If he lives in London or somewhere near, he gives an hour's talk in Darlington at the cost of two days' work, and though Darlington may be rewarding him generously for his hour's talking, it does nothing to make up for the loss of those two days. It would be much simpler—and equally just —to ask the publishers, those rich careless fellows, for free copies of all the author's books for each member of the society.

A world that is silly enough to invite actresses to write articles can hardly be expected to refrain from asking authors to talk in public. It remains, however, a gigantic absurdity. When I refuse to lecture, it is partly because I do not wish to inflict pain upon myself, but it is also because I do not wish to inflict pain upon others. I do not know what other authors are like when they are lecturing

« 69 »

—I never go to hear them—but I do know that I myself am completely insufferable. When I am lecturing, I dislike and despise the town I am in, the hall, the chairman, the audience, the subject— and myself. I have, I know, nearly all the worst mannerisms of a public speaker. I am at once shy and arrogant. I drone and croak and wheeze and gasp and cough and splutter and growl and shriek and scowl and grin and sweat and blush. My friends and relatives would not be paid to attend any lecture of mine. If I went on an American tour, as it has been sometimes suggested (probably out of malice) that I should do, there would be men with sawn-off shot-guns waiting for me outside the first hall. I have probably lost a hundred readers for the rest of my life every time I have given a lecture, except at those places where there were only about twenty people to hear me. I am not at all apologetic about this. I have never pretended to be a lecturer. If I possessed a handsome and ingratiating presence, a charming and cunningly modulated voice, probably I should not be a writer at all; I should be on the stage, which must be more fun than staying at home trying to add sentence to sentence. Give me a pile of quarto sheets, a fountain pen or a portable typewriter,

thing of his pleasure to the listeners. He is so
obviously enjoying himself that they cannot help
enjoying him too. In the same way, the bad lecturer, the awkward scowling croaking fellow, com-
municates his distaste for the business. His tones
of voice, his grimaces, his whole appearance, what
are they doing but indicating plainly the folly of
lecturing? I believe that half a dozen of us, thoroughly bad lecturers, could stop the thing if we
went about the country for a year, talking every
night. Twenty or thirty of us, if we pledged ourselves to it, could cure the American Middle-West
in one good winter. After we had gone, nobody
would ever want to hear a lecture again, and in a
decade or two the lecturer would be a quaint
ghost, like an alchemist or a torturer.

I wish now that some members of the last generation of authors had put this plan into practice.
Having written these columns on lectures and lecturing, the two I have promised to give seem much
nearer. The platform is only just round the corner. In a moment we shall have the chairman's
Opening Remarks and Few Words, during which
I shall sit in my uncomfortable chair, looking
brightly at nothing. Already my style is beginning
to wobble. It is not—er—that I've nothing left

to say—because—er—as a matter of fact I could go on talking—I mean writing—all night, that is, pages and pages—on this subject of—er—lectures, which is—or, rather—has always seemed, appeared, presented itself, to me as one which—one that—er—has always been one that has not only —er—had a great attraction, appealed to me, for many reasons—and—I mean, but—is really of immense importance because—that is—er—particularly at the present time, ladies and gentlemen.

Alas!—why did I promise? Why did I not conjure up the Everlasting Nay? To—er—is human, to refuse—divine.

I SAW the sign up a side-street: Madame Dash—Palmist. I decided at once to have my character, my destiny, unveiled. The way led up a narrow flight of stairs, shared by a number of people such as Poppleworth & Sons, Surveyors, and J. G. Burton & Co., Enquiry Agents. At first I could not find Madame Dash. There was no door bearing her name. I went up three flights of stairs that were narrower and dustier at every turn, and I found and refound Poppleworth & Sons and J. G. Burton & Co., but no Madame Dash. I returned to the street and looked up at the windows. One of them was draped in lace curtains. There, I told myself—and J. G. Burton could not have done better—there is Madame Dash. I climbed the stairs again, discovered the door that seemed to be nearest to the lace curtains, knocked, and was asked to enter.

The room was very dim because the end nearest the window had been partitioned off. A head appeared round the curtain of the partition and said: 'D'you want a reading? Just wite a mowment, please.' So I sat down in the remains of a leather arm-chair and waited in the dim room, which was very stuffy and reeked of cheap incense. I examined its four vases of artificial flowers and its two prints, *The Star of Bethlehem* and *Westward Bound: with the Compliments of the Canadian Shipping Line*. I sat there not one minute but ten, during which time there was a continual whispering behind the partition. Then at last two subdued-looking middle-aged women, who, I will swear, kept little sweets and tobacco shops and had husbands who disappeared ten years ago, crept round the curtain, and I was invited to take their place near the window, with Madame.

There was nothing of the alluring or sinister sibyl about Madame, who was short, plump, middle-aged, with a round red face and eyeglasses drolly supported by a very snub little nose. She was wearing a black dress and a rather dirty grey woollen jersey without sleeves, and looked like the owner of a cheap seaside boarding-house who occasionally attended meetings of the local Theosophical Society in winter. She had, however, a pleasant open face, and out of hours, with another sympathetic middle-aged woman and a cup of tea or a bottle of stout by her side, no doubt she would prove to be a very genial companion. At the moment, however, she was earnestness itself. She faced me across a little table, gave me a crystal, told me to cover it with my hands and think about those affairs that I wished her to discuss. Then she looked at my left hand. 'Well, yes, of course,' she began. It was just as if we had been talking for hours. Her voice had plunged straight into an easy, intimate tone. A very clever opening, I thought it.

'Well, yes, of course,' she said, 'you've always been sensitive and reserved, and so of course you've been misunderstood. You've reely an affectionate niture, but people don't think so. Thet's how it is with you. And you've lost fythe. You're one as can see through people. You know what's at the beck of their minds when they're talking to you, you know if they're lying, if they're guilty or not. But being sow reserved, it's got you misunderstood a good deal, it has. And then you've lost your fythe. You follow me, downcher?'

This, extended afterwards to 'You follow me now, downcher?' was her favourite phrase, and sometimes she put it in sadly, sometimes it came out briskly, sometimes it arrived with a triumphant ring. What she would do without it, I cannot imagine, for it served all manner of purposes. It kept me nodding like a mandarin. So far I agreed with everything she said. Her view of my character was singularly like my own.

It was now the turn of my right hand. 'Yes,' she said, 'you've had to work hard, but up to now you've not had all you've been entitled to have from your work. Other people been getting the benefit. You follow me, downcher? People have picked your brains before to-day. Professional, aren't you? It's written here in your hand that you're professional. You'll do better this year than you've ever done before. The months of My and June'll be good for you, specially good. You'll arrive at a position of great responsibility, you will, before long. Up to now, though you might have done fairly well, you reely haven't had your chance. You follow me, downcher?'

Yes, I was following her. All these were, emphatically, my sentiments. At the moment I could not think of the names of the rascals who had been picking my brains and stealing the fruits of my endeavour, but I had no doubt at all that they existed.

'And another thing,' Madame pursued. 'Anybody looking at you would think you were a gentleman who had the best of health, but you haven't, you know, reely. You've not been as well as you might have been since last November, nothing like so well as you look. You see what I mean?'

I agreed with enthusiasm. It is perfectly true that I am hardly ever as well as I look, and I have the misfortune to be surrounded by people— relatives, friends, and even doctors—who simply cannot understand this, who do not realize what I suffer in my own quietude.

She had finished with my hands now, and began gazing into the crystal I had been holding. 'I see a Nightch,' she announced, impressively. 'A Nightch!' I cried, startled. 'Yes, the letter Ightch,' she said. 'D'you know anybody whose nime begins with a Nightch?' But this did not take us far because I know so many people whose names begin with that letter. She mentioned several other initial letters too, but this was easily the least valuable part of the séance. I refused to take an interest in these vague alphabetical creatures.

'I see money coming to you from two directions,' she said, peering in the crystal. 'It's in here, two different directions. Can you understand what that means? It's money coming to you soon.'

I am accustomed to seeing money depart in all directions, but the thought of it coming, two shining streams converging upon me, was new and distinctly pleasant. I did not understand what it meant (or if I did, I do not see why I should tell everybody), but for a moment I enjoyed the thrill of one about to be rich.

'I see a tall gentleman, very straight he is—he stands up in here—oldish gentleman, and he means well to you. You can trust him. And there's a younger gentleman, dark with a thin fice, and he's to be trusted too. And these two'll bring you in a lot of money. And you're doing a lot of signing, a lot of signing. You follow me, downcher?' 'Well,' I said, hesitantly, 'as a matter or fact, I always have a good deal of signing to do.' 'But we don't see here anything you do the ordinary way of things,' she said. 'This is special signing, something that'll please you.' She stared again in silence for a few moments. 'You're in a city with narrow streets and very tall buildings, you've had to go there on business, and it's very lucky for you. Very narrow streets and very tall buildings. Liverpool or Manchester, p'raps.'

'I hope not,' I murmured. It is one thing to be told you are to be lucky in some strange city, and it is quite another thing to be told you will be in Liverpool or Manchester. I felt disappointed, but clung to the hope that topography was not her strong point.

Her next remark was rather reassuring. 'The streets mayn't be so narrow,' she observed, 'because it may be only the buildings that are so high. Anyhow I see you there, and it'll be lucky for you.' Which left me with a conviction that the city was New York, that I was to be there signing contracts for plays, films, serial stories, short stories, five hundred dollar articles on The American Woman as I See Her, with men straight as ramrods standing by, looking after my interests. 'Now, you can ask me anything you like,' she said, but really by this time I felt there was little to ask. After a minute or two, during which she told me again that I was reserved, sensitive, affectionate, misunderstood, witty and keen-brained, unlucky so far but about to be very successful, and that all I wanted was a little fythe, I did put a question, but it was only to ask her what I owed her. 'It's half a crown, that is, if you're satisfied,' she replied.

Satisfied! I should think I was. Without knowing my age or profession, anything of my personal history, she had yet contrived to tell me all the things that I want to be told, the things I have always secretly believed to be true of myself and that nobody but me—and this kindly oracle—ever seemed to understand. The session was worth a hundred half-crowns. It was a day-dream of one-self suddenly conjured into an oracular utterance. It was a visit to a magic mirror.

As I went out, I saw two people waiting their turn. I only had a glimpse of them, but it was enough to show me that they too would prove to be reserved, affectionate, sensitive, misunderstood, unfortunate perhaps up to now but about to rush into prosperity, immense good fortune. I thought of them pleasantly as I passed the doors of Pop-pleworth & Sons, Surveyors, and J. G. Burton & Co., Enquiry Agents, and descended into the world again.

THE CARDS

WHAT has happened to the playing cards in Russia? Is the old bourgeois pack still allowed, or are people winning tricks there with the Commissar of trumps? Perhaps trumps are forbidden, being something of a bourgeois device. Perhaps the suits have been changed, probably into spades, hammers, revolvers, bombs. And what about the old hierarchy? If nothing has been done yet, I suggest the following reforms: the Knave to be Local Soviet Representative; the Queen to be Female Secretary at Headquarters; the King to be Commissar; the Ace to be simply Tcheka. What a satisfaction there would be in crashing down the Tcheka of bombs! Here is another and better reform, which would convert the pastime into good propaganda and remove from it any taint of the old bourgeois ideas. Keep three of the suits as they are, but make the fourth into a fully class-conscious proletarian revolutionary communistic suit, with its own proper hierarchy, and establish this suit as perpetual trumps. Thus every game over which the comrades unbent their minds would illustrate the ultimate triumph of the masses, chiefly, of course, in the persons of the Local Soviet Representative, Female Secretary at Headquarters, and Commissar, with Tcheka, very rightly, above all, a symbol of liberty triumphant.

It may well be, though, that before long these monarchs of the cards will be the only royal personages left in the world. Even now they are certainly the ones we know best. The Queen of Spades has more reality than the Queen of Spain. I do not know the King of Italy even by sight, but I am familiarly acquainted with the King of Clubs. I could write a book, on the model of those written by retired diplomats, entitled *Memories of Four Courts,* and might even contrive to fake a facsimile letter or two, as illustrations, purporting to be from the Queen of Diamonds and the King of Spades. Quite truthfully, I could describe how their highnesses of Clubs had always been very kind to me, frequently putting themselves and a large number of their subjects at my disposal, and how, unfortunately, the Clubs' prestige was so low that I had gained little from their generosity. I could wind up with a little scandal, something *entre nous*, about the Knave of Hearts, that amusing fellow with whom I have spent many a merry evening. And, after all, I really have spent many a merry evening with him and his fellow Knaves and their respective masters and mistresses. Anyone who can play with these kings and queens, pasteboard though they are, year after year and not find them coming, if only faintly, to life, taking on personality, must be singularly unimaginative. We are always being compelled by the newspapers to read about the opinions and whims and habits of people in whom we have no interest whatever, and so I am not going to apologize for discussing these grand personages of the pack. They at least are of our acquaintance.

A friend of mine, who does not write as often as he ought, once produced an essay noting and defending the superiority of Spades, and I only wish this essay were at hand so that I could challenge him. There was, I fear, a touch of snobbery there, a hint of that worship of mere success which is so prevalent nowadays. I have never been able to discern any marks of real superiority in Spades. It is true they have prospered of late and on most occasions are accepted as the most powerful suit, but this is the result of certain arbitrary strokes of fortune rather than of any deciding merit in the Spades themselves. Perhaps I am a trifle prejudiced against them. They have always seemed to me an unfriendly, even sinister suit. I have never liked the look of the King, a cold, crafty, implacable fellow, loving nothing but power. You never see him unbending, never catch a twinkle in his eyes. How stiffly, rigidly, he holds his little sword! You feel that it is there as a symbol of his power and not as a glorious plaything, with which to cut and slash and make bright passes. When war has been declared, you will not find him at the front, leading his troops, but somewhere in the rear, coldly plotting in the tiny shadow of that raised sword. It is not that he lacks courage, but he has no dash, no spirit of adventure; he is merely so much merciless will and brain; he is a king without a heart. In the Palace of Spades there is no laughter. The Queen looks even colder and craftier than her lord, another Catherine de Medici. Even the Knave has no trace of good humour in his face, which wears a perpetual cold sneer. No, I do not like these Spades, and no matter how fortune may favour them, no matter how their prestige may soar, I shall contest their superiority.

In pleasant contrast to these cold and sinister personages are their neighbours, the open-handed, frank and affable Clubs. It is the scandal of the pack that these excellent people should be frequently rated so low, even lower—to our shame be it said—than the contemptible Diamonds. For the King himself I have nothing but affectionate praise. It does one good to see his honest open manly countenance. There is not a better companion in the pack. He may have his limitations as a ruler. I will not disguise the fact that a little more brain would improve him, for he is too often outwitted by his fellow monarchs, particularly him of Spades, and is too apt to take everything at its face value. But he never fails to lead his men (a rather ragged and badly-equipped set they are, too, I am afraid) and is as brave in the field as he is affable in the audience chamber. He has undoubtedly the best appearance of any of the Kings, not more handsome than Hearts perhaps (Spades and Diamonds need not be considered) but less foppish, more manly. His beard is not too carefully forked and combed, and there is pleasant roguery in his little curling moustache. His clothes would pass Polonius himself, being regal 'but not expressed in fancy; rich, not gaudy'; they are brighter than those of Spades, but without the frippery of ermine that you find in Hearts or the cloth of gold and glittering braid of Diamonds. His lady is in every respect worthy of him; a charming and sensible woman, handsome too, though perhaps a little too long in the nose for all tastes. The Knave is younger than the other Knaves and consequently is somewhat undeveloped, but he seems a pleasant, thoughtful lad, not at all embittered as yet by the spectacle of the declining fortunes of the Clubs.

Hearts I put somewhere between the Clubs and the Spades. The King is an amusing fellow, but, of course, something of a dandy and a swashbuckler. Notice how he carries his sword, holding it up behind his head as if ready to strike. This is sheer gasconading. It is well known that when the moment arrives he is never a very eager swordsman. On a fair field with no favour, Clubs would make mincemeat of him. Notice, too, his elaborately curled beard and hair, and the shaven upper lip—a dandiacal touch. How characteristic, too, is the position of his right hand, too flabby for the swordsman he pretends to be, for it is obviously smoothing the ermine fringe on his gaudy robe! He is trying to look perfectly debonair and at ease, but he cannot keep a faint hint of worry out of his face. He is, of course, frightened of his wife, the handsomest woman in the pack but—as they say—a handful. The Knave, with his yellow curls, his supercilious moustache, and his scented leaf, which he is for ever smelling, is no better than his mistress, and if space allowed I could set down some very queer little stories about him. There are good reasons, then, why I cannot admire the Hearts, yet they must be admitted to be far better company than the Spades or the Diamonds. Once a few affectations are ignored, the King can be at times an excellent companion, and his Queen and Knave are capable of providing good comedy for the intelligent spectator. We have had many a crazy night at the court of Hearts.

For the Diamonds I have nothing but contempt. It is, I repeat, a scandal that they should ever take precedence of the Clubs. The King himself is a crafty and cowardly miser. It is typical of him that he alone of the Kings should have his face perpetually turned away from us. Unlike the others, he does not grasp a sword, but has his hand outstretched, as if in prayer. That is his hypocrisy. You will notice that behind him is a weapon that has a marked resemblance to a headman's axe—a very significant fact, that. He reminds us of Louis XI. The Queen, a figure stiff with gold braid, is cold and proud. Even the Knave looks sullen and suspicious, and, in spite of his fine clothes, we cannot help suspecting that he is badly paid and probably victualled on cold mutton and small beer. Even the most paradoxical of my friends would never dream of asserting the superiority of Diamonds. They were clearly intended to be the lowest of the suits, with Spades coming a little above them; then Hearts should take the next place; and highest of all, leading the procession round the green-topped tables, the frank and friendly Clubs. It is to them, in their present misfortune, that I dedicate this essay.

A FISH IN BAYSWATER

THE other morning found me walking down Queen's Road, Bayswater, in a deep fit of depression. I cannot remember now why I was feeling so depressed, and I do not suppose that I knew at the time. These are the days when we weep and know not why. Not Bass nor Worthington nor all the foaming brewage of the world shall ever medicine us to that sweet peace that we knew yesterday. We may assume that I had discovered either that I was not fit for life or that life was not fit for me. I usually incline towards the latter view, and when I am out of spirits I see myself as a baffled idealist, betrayed by the very nobility of my mind, in short, as Hamlet in modern dress. The fact that the mood may not have its root cause in the mind at all, and the further fact that I smoke too much and take too little exercise, I generally contrive to overlook. Some people, whose digestive processes happen to be excellent, advise you to search for the cause during the actual fit of depression and assure you that once the cause is found the mood will pass. Such

« 91 »

people, however, forget that you will probably be too depressed to examine yourself, for at such times nothing is worth the trouble it involves. Even the psycho-analyst would make no headway because his first conviction in this state would be that psycho-analysis was useless. Knowing how blasphemous we can become at these moments, I can even imagine him damning the Unconscious. But let us return to Queen's Road, Bayswater, down which I strolled the other morning, telling myself that all things were stale, flat and unprofitable.

Something happened there that changed my mood completely. At one moment life had seemed no better than the stirring of withered leaves against a grey wall, so much drudgery and so many pin-pricks, a bore's interminable tale. The next moment it was as if a curtain had been whisked up, revealing the true scene of things; and I knew that life was as rich as a plum-pudding, that it had entertainment enough to keep us amused though we should live a million years and travel from here to Aldebaran. Not only was I no longer depressed, but I was suddenly excited and happy. After stopping a moment, I swung away and swaggered down the rest of Queen's Road as jauntily as if I had just been given a thousand pounds. What had happened? Is there magic in Bayswater? I can tell you what happened, but I cannot say whether there is any magic in the Queen's Road. It chanced that I came to a fish-monger's shop, putting out a delightful cool reek of the foreshore, and no sooner had my nose caught the smell of it than my eye caught sight of the wet marble slab and the packed ice and, there in the middle, a very large flat fish. I stopped short for a second—you must see me staring out of the grey wilderness of my low spirits—to look at this fish.

The fish itself is not important. I do not know what kind of fish it was, and can only say that it was very large, and very flat, and unusually fishy. The point is, though, that when I saw that fish I immediately thought of the sea. I do not mean that I merely said to myself 'The sea!' or was visited by a fleeting image of waves and foam. It was much more intense than that, as if the fish had instantly pulled me into the sea. Not that I really felt I was in the sea, but I had a momentary vision, rich and bewildering as a pageant, of the sea. There came to me, in one glorious rush, thoughts and images of white cliffs on our South Coast, the Yorkshire caves and coves I knew as a

boy, great Atlantic rollers a day out from the
Azores, Conrad's *Typhoon*, spray shooting over
Cornish rocks, the overture to the *Flying Dutch-
man*, the smell of drying sea-weed and the feel of
sand between my toes, the flying fish in the Car-
ibbean, Melville's *Moby Dick*, a five-masted sailing ship in the Baltic, the first few bars of the
Hebrides, a glimpse of the Mediterranean blue between the pines, tiny crabs in the pools along the
shore, salt-crusted tramp steamers swaying past
Lundy, the melancholy wash of a quiet sea, the
brief epic of the Clippers, fish slithering out at
Grimsby, the phosphorescent sea I saw one night
off Antwerp, seagulls circling over the white foam
astern, a mid-Atlantic storm smashing against the
deadlights, a night of fog and hooting on the
Dogger, Gibraltar catching the early morning sunshine, old boats on the beach and the rusted sup-
ports of a pier, my sand castles crumbling in the
tides of long ago.

Now I am not prepared to say that all this
flashed through my mind as I halted a moment
before that fish in the Queen's Road. Yet I think
it possible that that sudden vision contained even
more than I have set down. The point is that only
by producing some such list as that can I suggest

what happened in my mind. The sight of that fish brought before me the sea, the whole colossal thing, and whatever my memory brought back to me, whatever associations came by way of books and music and art, were there, making up something that was not really a thought so much as a rich and confused feeling, or, if you like, a vision. That curtain which had been lowered between life and me during my fit of depression had suddenly been lifted to let me catch a glimpse of the sea, and once I had caught that glimpse the whole curtain was no more and my depression was at an end. This was, you see, no common glimpse, a peep through the misty spectacles of custom, but a sudden flashing vision, a brief acquaintance with what we might call the thing-in-itself, even though it was tangled with all manner of personal memories and associations. No sooner had it flashed through my mind than I felt a little rush of ecstasy. I hugged with delight the thought of the sea-ishness of the sea. Immediately, then, the lights went up everywhere and all life was rich and strange and a marvel, and I was out of spirits no longer.

These moments are essentially moments of aesthetic vision, and it is out of them that literature and art and music are produced. The thing is happening all the time. It is not necessary that you should be in love with the subject of the little vision, though real indifference to it is probably fatal. There must, I think, be feeling there, and dislike will do as well as affection. The stuff of which these things are made, of course, comes out of our actual memories of real experiences and talks and books and art in general. Somebody says 'France' to me or I meet the word in some idle context, and immediately I see long straight roads, green shutters folded back, tables under trees, bearded citizens making their way to the little café in the square, and all the rest of it. At least, that is how I am compelled to describe what happens, but actually I do not see a series of little pictures but somehow entertain a large confused idea that could be translated into these pictures and that gives me the feeling of having seen them. Once again, the France-ishness of this France gives me enormous pleasure, and immediately I am visited by the thought that life itself, the whole thing, and not merely France or the sea or whatever began it, is wonderful, a miracle of variety, richness, splendour. And the goodness and badness of things is not considered: at these times you are, as it were, sitting on top of the Tree of Knowledge and not eating of the fruit below. You are, too, completely disinterested, and must be to have the experience. Thus, it would be impossible for me to have such a vision of the contemporary literary scene, just as it would be impossible, I imagine, for the second engineer of a liner or the director of a trawling company to share my vision of the sea. This is one reason why the enthusiastic money-maker, the financier with his finger in all manner of pies, pays heavily for his wealth and power: he misses such a lot of fun inside.

Setting aside personal relationships (and even they can become part of this experience), I should say that this aesthetic experience constitutes the most intense and enduring pleasure we know in life. It is an art that is going on all the time in our heads. Out of it, as I suggested before, come the arts themselves, which are based on the wonder that lights these fleeting visions. It is quite likely that the artist on the whole finds a more intense pleasure in this kind of experience than the ordinary person, though I am convinced that it is something else, namely, the gift of expression, that really makes the artist. He is the man who can do something with this experience, not merely the man who enjoys it; he can put out a hand and catch the fluttering thing and then set it winging in the outside world, so that we may all see it, sharing his ecstasy. And that, I think, is enough. Another step—and I shall be producing aesthetics. There was a time when I read and thought about nothing but aesthetics, but once I had recovered I swore that I would never approach the subject again. But if ever I weaken and bring out a thesis, I feel sure that it will open most strangely—with a fish in Bayswater.

CRUMPY

IS THE democratic system of authorship nearing its end? Is the patron to be revived? These queries are not so absurd as they may appear at the first glance. I have heard more than one author declare himself in favour of the patron as opposed to the general public, though I must confess that I have never found the arguments very convincing. There is ample scope for decent patronage under present conditions. If a wealthy man admires the work of a young poet and wishes to show his appreciation, there is no reason why he should not buy three hundred copies of the poet's latest volume, thereby doubling its sale. The only reason why this does not happen very frequently is not because wealthy men have never thought of this obvious method of encouraging young poets and have turned away, figures of baffled benevolence, but because in these days wealthy men have not the slightest desire to encourage young poets. Yet there is, I think, some signs of a move towards a modified form of patronage. It is seen in the growing practice of publishing limited, signed, expensive editions of new books, which give an author's admirers an opportunity of showing that he is worth more to them than Tom, Dick, or Harry. Perhaps we may soon see a return to the old subscription method of publishing, so that once more our volumes of new verse will be furnished with long lists of patrons: Thos. Jackson, Esq., one copy; Miss James and Miss Georgiana James, three copies; Rev. Augustus Johnson, two copies; Colonel Jones, one copy. This is at least an honest and dignified proceeding, and it has given to the world some masterpieces in its time.

If there is to be patronage again, I hope it will be something of this kind, and not something a thousand times more vulgar than the most catchpenny appeal to the general public. Are we to develop our own up-to-date system of patronage? An advertisement in the Personal Column of *The Times* suggests that we are. It ran: 'Author, of historic name, will inscribe new work (classic edition) to Patron for £1,000.' There is all the brutal directness of Big Business here. No timid and foolish shilly-shallying, hinting that in return for some necessary help the author would be willing to show his gratitude, etc., etc. No, the bargain is frankly stated: a dedication for £1,000.

The terms seem to me rather high. For my own part, I would not sell a dedication, but if any gentleman cared to let me have a cheque for £250, I think I should find that the relation between us was of such a nature that it naturally led to my dedicating my next book to him. It is true, of course, that I have not an historic name. Probably you are justified in asking a thousand pounds if you have an historic name. I wonder who our author is? Surely it would not be difficult to discover his identity when the historic names in contemporary literature could easily be counted on one's fingers. And what does he mean by 'classic edition'? When is a new book a 'classic edition'? Why 'classic'? a horrible adjective! Is it possible that, in their limited and august circle, these personages with historic names talk of their classic editions, knowing full well that, unlike you and me, they can afford to use such phrases?

How many replies has our author received? It would be so interesting to know that I think I would try to bribe the advertising staff if the paper were any other than *The Times*. (And what a great deal those people, who tabulate the replies to the Personal Column appeals, must know about human nature!) For the life of me I cannot even begin to guess what the response will be. All that I know is that the one person who, if he had seen this appeal, would certainly have answered it, has vanished from the world. This was Mr. Crump, who makes a brief but not unmemorable appearance in the *Life and Letters of Lord Macaulay*. We are there given an extract from the journal of Lord Carlisle, dated February 14, 1852, on which day he met Macaulay at a dinner-party: 'He told us of two letters he had received from America—one from a Mr. Crump, offering him 500 dollars if he could introduce the name of Crump into his History; another from a Young Men's Philosophical Society in New York, beginning, "Possibly our fame has not pinioned the Atlantic." ' I am glad that the fame of Mr. Crump has pinioned both the Atlantic and the years. He shall have his little mention here—for what it is worth—for nothing, when the last of those dollars vanished long ago. Mr. Crump is worth examining. He is almost a symbolic figure. We could coin out of him an adjective that is missing from our vocabulary, and one that is very necessary now because the attitude of mind it describes is greatly in evidence. Nowhere is it more in evidence than in the country of Mr. Crump's origin. Indeed, crumpiness is an American trait.

How shall we describe this crumpiness? Let us return to Mr. Crump himself. Obviously there is, behind this extraordinary offer of his, a most unusual and droll inconsistency. There are to be discovered in his mind, working together most inharmoniously, a fine idealism and a most gross materialism. He shows himself capable at one and the same time of rising higher than the common level and falling sadly below it. I do not believe for one moment that his motive was a base one, that he merely came to the conclusion that the appearance of his name in Macaulay's History would be, shall we say, a means of advertising his wares. No, he wanted his name in because he had a vast admiration for Macaulay and his History. He saw that massive work marching triumphantly down the years, for ever adding to its laurels. Decay and death and oblivion could not touch such a masterpiece. A host of readers would be exclaiming in wonder and delight at these volumes when he, Mr. Crump, was dead and gone, perhaps when all trace of him had vanished, when the very name itself was nothing but a fantastic rumour. As he saw volume after volume of the History beginning their immortal progress, he also had a vision of the Crumps, filled with desires that immortality itself could only satisfy but remaining here only for their little day, with barely time to show what a Crump might do before the coming of the hurrying darkness:

> How fast has brother followed brother
> From sunshine to the sunless land!

Moved by the contrast between these two visions, he told himself that he would book a place, if a place only microscopic in size, in this great chariot of fame. As it rolled down the centuries, it should bear with it the name of Crump.

This is to rise above the common level. This is to have a noble love of literature, of fame. This is to be an idealist, one not living by bread alone. But no sooner does he take action than he displays the most astonishing and gross insensitiveness. He acts as if fame were a commodity that could be bought at so many dollars per pound, as if literature were something like the Chicago Stock Exchange, as if his admired great author were also a cheapjack. It does not occur to him that what Macaulay would not do for friendship or for fun, he would certainly not do for a handful of dollars.

And here, of course, is the extraordinary inconsistency of the man. His attitude is so contradictory that we cannot hope to understand him. If he had no sense of values, if he were a mere grubber, he would never dream of wanting to have his name mentioned in a volume of history; yet if he had any sense of values, if he were not a mere grubber, he would never dream of offering 500 dollars and buying the service. We cannot hope to understand such an attitude, but we can at least label it, particularly as it happens to be very common now. All such people are crumpy. They are obviously crumpy when they are able to combine two extreme attitudes towards Royalty, for example, contriving that a royal personage shall be at once an object of veneration and yet turned into a mountebank for their benefit. I do not know whether our author of *The Times* advertisement is crumpy or not, for it is quite possible that he is a cynic, only seeing historic names in the light of thousand pound dedications. But any person who closes with his offer, paying a thousand pounds for something that immediately becomes worthless just because it is bought and sold is certainly crumpy. The whole world, I suspect, is rapidly becoming crumpier.

THE DICKENS FAYRE

A DICKENS Folk Fayre and Pageant ought to to be crowded. Imagine Mr. Pickwick or Mrs. Gamp stepping forward to see rows of empty chairs, to hear nothing but a faint crackle of applause—a horrible picture! If the affair is to be really Dickensy, all the town must be there, eating and drinking and nodding and smiling and sweating and bustling and stamping and cheering. The Dickens Fayre to which I went last Thursday was as crowded as *Pickwick Papers*. Those of us who were late for the afternoon performance of the pageant had no hope of seats, and I for one did not see how I should even find standing room. However, I followed a very determined looking middle-aged man (perhaps it was Major Bagstock) along a corridor at the back of the hall, and at last found myself among the little tables set out for tea. There I had quite a good view of the stage, though I was always in danger of putting a hand in a plate of cakes when I absent-mindedly leaned back. This Fayre was in aid of the church, so the vicar was in charge. It was he who told us all about Dickens before the pageant began. 'One of the giants of the Victorian era,' he was saying when I arrived. When he had finished and, perspiring, smiling nervously, and making any number of mysterious signs, had taken his place below, standing near the edge of the platform, an old man with a short pipe in his mouth poked his head through the curtains at the side. This was clearly a signal for the little orchestra to play, for it started up at once, and after a minute or two the curtains began wobbling, drew away from one another, hesitated, then finally went creaking back, disclosing a desk in one corner of the stage, a desk with two candles burning on it and several large important volumes bound in calf. There was a figure seated at this desk. It was Dickens himself, flourishing a gigantic quill pen. We all applauded.

I found it difficult to hear what Dickens said, for he had a trick of talking into his beard. I do know, however, that he talked throughout in verse, and that this verse reminded me of the old opening scenes in pantomimes, when the demon and the fairy queen used to defy one another before plunging into a duet for baritone and soprano. (And I am certain that this is the kind of verse that Dickens would have chosen himself.) Dickens would speak several lines of his bad verse. The old man with the pipe would poke his head through the curtain at the side, and the orchestra would play a chord or two or a march. Then Dickens characters would appear, sometimes in a little procession, sometimes in a tableau at the back of the stage. The enthusiasm of the audience was tremendous, as well it might be, for everybody there was enjoying the pleasure of a twofold recognition. They had the pleasure of recognizing the various characters. They had the further pleasure of recognizing their friends and relatives in those poke bonnets and high felt hats. I was rather out of it because all the actors were strangers to me and I did not always hear what Dickens was saying. There was a number of sheepish young men in high felt hats who did not seem to represent anybody in particular, though I have no doubt they could be sorted out into Copperfields and Swivellers and Pips.

Most of the major characters seemed to have changed a little. Mr. Pickwick, for example, has apparently grown younger and younger: last Thursday he was only about thirty-five. Mrs. Gamp is far more respectable in appearance than she used to be. Mr. Micawber, I regret to say, was much thinner, and in place of that smooth and shining expanse of bald head he had a rather disgusting, wrinkled, yellow crown that looked suspiciously like painted canvas. Quilp was neither a dwarf nor deformed, but had the appearance of a young gentleman who preferred to spend his time looking for something on the floor. Bumble was not there: *he was impersonated by his wife;* it did not take me five seconds to discover that. Oliver Twist was there, bowl and all, and was obviously enjoying himself, but he looked strangely neat and clean and not unlike one of those page boys one sees at the big hotels. Bill Sykes had a rabbit half hidden under his coat and must have taken to poaching. Fagin and Scrooge and Uriah Heep have not changed at all, I am happy to say.

There was something queer about Sam Weller, but I did not discover what it was until the pageant proper was over and we were all strolling about in the grounds outside and the girls in their 1840 dresses (very pretty they looked too) were being photographed. It was then I noticed Sam Weller, who was wearing rimless eyeglasses and asking no less a person than Dickens himself to bring a cup of tea. The attitude, the tone of voice, told me all: Sam Weller was Dickens's wife. That was very odd. But then, it seemed to me that outside there, when all the actors were smoking their pipes, the girls giggling at the photographer, the women becoming expansive over cups of tea, merry old men bowling for a pig, Mr. Pickwick getting in everybody's way, and the vicar trying to be in four places at once, it seemed to me then that it was all far more like Dickens than the pageant was. The moment some of these good souls stopped pretending to be Dickens characters, they really became Dickens characters. If I had caught a glimpse of the great man himself bowling for a pig, I should not have been surprised.

That is not to say that the pageant was a failure. It was a gigantic success. The vicar announced that, contrary to the programme, it would be given again in the evening, a fact that speaks for itself. There was not a character that did not get its round of applause. Even Edwin Drood, a vague young gentleman who stood at the back of the stage, raised his arms, and looked as if he were about to be sick, was enthusiastically welcomed. As for the Pickwicks and Micawbers and Gamps, they were recognized at once and rapturously applauded. Indeed, one old gentleman standing near me stamped so hard that he became a menace to the whole building. These people were not only seeing their friends in a masquerade but they were seeing those other old friends from the vast dream-world of Dickens and were clapping their hands at the sight of them. Consider what this means. You get together a few hundred ordinary people of a small town, and all of them recognize this novelist's characters at a glance. Only recently M. Maurois told us that one of the things that astonished him in England was the sight of an actor in a music-hall very successfully entertaining his audience by giving impersonations of Dickens characters. It could not happen in France, he observed, for there no characters of fiction are so well known. But if you want still better evidence of the astounding fame of Dickens, you have it here in this pageant and Fayre.

If there were statues of this man in every square in London, this little pageant would still be better evidence of his fame. Strictly speaking, there has not been a famous writer since Dickens. Everybody knows about Mr. Bernard Shaw, we say, and most people do know his name, but that is only because they have seen it so often in the papers. Ask ninety-nine people out of every hundred who John Tanner is and they will stare at you. Kipps and Mr. Polly, Clayhanger and Denry Machin, Soames Forsythe—who are these people? Not one person in a hundred, perhaps two hundred, perhaps five, could tell you, and yet we imagine that everybody knows Wells, Bennett, Galsworthy.

I wish somebody would stand at the corner of a London street and put a question or two about authors to every passer-by. I have met educated people, who were in the habit of using libraries and called themselves readers, and they did not know the names of some of our best living poets and novelists. To understand the colossal fame of Dickens you have to go outside literature altogether now: Charlie Chaplin is the only rival worth considering. But is this kind of fame worth having? Of course it is, and worth more than all the statues, titles, dedications, memorials, commentators, volumes of *So-and-so and his Age*, put together. And here is a question for those fellow scribblers who do not like these innocent remarks, who are even now bridling and putting on peevish airs. Who said that every man should sit down to write as if he had a million readers? Was it said yesterday by Nat Gould, or to-day by Ethel M. Dell? No, it was said the day before yesterday, by Goethe.

COMMERCIAL INTERLUDE

I AM staying in an hotel in a Midland town, and it has turned me into a Commercial. When I arrived yesterday—that is, when I walked down the road from the station—I saw that the hotel called itself Family and Commercial, but as soon as I had spent five minutes in the place I realized that it was purely Commercial. It cannot have seen a family for twenty years. But Commercial is no idle boast. The coffee-room was full of Commercials and I became one myself simply by engaging a room here. 'Is there a place,' I asked the maid, 'where I can sit and write in the morning?' 'Just the Coffee-Room—for Commercials,' she replied. I am still wondering what would have happened if I had said that I was not Commercial but Family. (And, after all, I can easily prove that I am more of a family man than a commercial one.) Would rooms shuttered and shrouded these twenty years have been thrown open for me? Would the Boots have gone round blowing the dust from Family armchairs? The maid, however, never hesitated a moment: I was obviously a Commercial.

Her method of reasoning, I imagine, was that no man who was not a Commercial would ever dream of staying at this hotel. No doubt, too, I have the look of a bagman, one of the less prosperous kind, travelling in some antiquated line of fancy goods. (And there are times when I see myself in that melancholy part.) For the moment, then, I am a Commercial. I sleep in Number Eight, and eat, drink, smoke, read, write, in the coffee-room; and I am trying to summon up courage to cry, very loudly and snappily as the others do, "Good-morning, gentlemen!" 'Good-evening, gentlemen!' I hope to bring it off once before I go. Already I am being regarded with suspicion because I mumble the greeting and leave out the 'gentlemen.' The other Commercials are probably asking one another what the place is coming to.

That is a question I can answer. If all the other bedrooms are like mine—and I see no reason why they shouldn't be—then the hotel is tottering into ruin. My room is reasonably clean, but that exhausts its virtues. It is as cheerful as the interior of an old trunk that has been put away in the box-room these fifteen years. Its ancient wallpaper is

« 115 »

faded and stained beyond recognition as a colour or a pattern; in one corner there is plaster wandering across, like a river on a huge map; and high up the wall opposite my bed the damp seems to have crumbled away paper, plaster and all. The two windows, which look out upon the backs of warehouses but occasionally offer a glimpse of a passing tram, are draped with yellowed lace curtains and very old blue roller blinds. Last night I could not persuade the blinds to stay down and this morning I had an even greater difficulty in cajoling them up again.

The toilet set is chipped, cracked, or broken. The jug has no spout. The soap-dish is completely severed into two halves. And there is a certain missing handle that cannot even be discussed. In the corner by the washstand is a row of coathooks, but most of the hooks are either leaning forward at a ridiculous angle or are not there at all, and anyhow you cannot hang your clothes over a washstand. The bed is very high and very lumpy and very cold. Climbing into it is not going to bed but to Tibet. The single electric light is in a distant corner, removed as far as possible from the bed, the washstand, the mirror. A notice informs you that 'The electric light will be turned off at

11.30 p.m. Candles are placed in each bedroom, and the first statement is true. The candles, I suspect, went out with the Family. The only towel you receive is a very small face towel, and so far as I can see, any other would be useless. The Commercial apparently is supposed to take a bath whenever he returns to his distant home. This hotel sees the Commercial as a man who almost completes his dressing on first rising, shaves and washes his face and hands in the pint of warmish water brought to him, and after that does nothing but a little rinsing and dabbing with cold water and a slimy face towel.

I have never occupied a prison cell, but I imagine it to be rather more cheerless than this bedroom of mine. But I defy any other kind of apartment to compete with it in desolating discomfort. The moment you arrive, it announces: 'I am simply so many cubic feet of bedroom space. My little iron grate has never had a fire in it and never will have. Nobody here has ever really looked at me, given me a thought. The sooner my walls crumble away, the better.' And when you return at night—and in Midland towns you return quite early—the room is even more expressive: 'I'm a chill and cheerless hole,' it cries at once. 'Nobody has ever really lived in me. Get to sleep immediately—if you can. But listen to those trams, groaning and groaning away. Plenty of noise here, isn't there? Not a cheerful noise though. What d'you think of life, eh? Care for it much? You're a damned fool to be sober, if you ask me. Trying to read, eh? Haven't seen much of that, I must say, but it won't work. Lights out soon, you know. Cold, isn't it? You're not so young as you were, are you? Getting many orders, business good? I thought not.'

Something like that, I will swear, it said to me last night, when I turned in at the early hour of ten-thirty. I had been to the local Hippodrome, where I had been saddened by the spectacle of a fifth-rate revue, a show without a single gleam of talent or high spirits, simply so many over-worked and under-dressed girls and hoarse-voiced and perspiring men. I had had a drink downstairs in the public smoking-room where the usual semi-circle of patrons were drearily chaffing the fat bar-maid. Then I tried the coffee-room, joining the three Commercials who were sitting round the little fire at the far end of the room.

There was the young man in blue laboriously reading the *Daily Mirror*; the red-faced man in brown, who was yawning over a glass of stout; and the elderly bald man who sucked an empty pipe and did nothing else until the maid came in, whereupon he brightened up and addressed her as Minnie. I could see that bald man going round, year after year, to all the commercial hotels in England, calling the maid Minnie here, Gertie at Nottingham, Mabel at Leicester, Gladys at Birmingham. I filled a pipe and stared in front of me, first at the fire, then at the two monstrous engravings, *The Jubilee Celebration in Westminster Abbey, June* 21, 1887, and *Ramsgate Sands (circa* 1850), and when I had tired of these, at a glass case of stuffed humming-birds perched upon a gilt tree. I remember thinking how incredible it was that there really were places where such creatures, gorgeous in vermilion and sea-green and amethyst, were alive, actually flying about. (We Commercials have the oddest thoughts sometimes.) The young man in blue still pored over his *Daily Mirror*; the red-faced man produced wider and wider yawns; the elderly one sank into an apathetic pipe-sucking again; and outside the Midland trams departed noisily and lugubriously into the deeper night of the suburbs. So I went up to my room, and when I heard what it had to say, I told myself that I would never even hint a fault in commercial travellers again.

Fortunately, I had a book with me. It was Adlington's translation of *The Golden Ass*. About eleven o'clock, when a little warmth was creeping down towards my toes, I was reading the following passage: 'And so, in this sort I went to supper, and behold I found at Byrrhena's house a great company of strangers, and of the chief and principall of the city: the beds, made of Citron and Ivory, were richly adorned and spred with cloath of gold, the Cups were garbished pretiously, and there were divers other things of sundry fashion, but of like estimation and price: here stood a glasse gorgeously wrought, there stood another of Christall finely painted. There stood a cup of glittering silver, and here stood another of shining gold, and here was another of amber artificially carved and made with pretious stones. Finally, there was all things that might be desired: the servitors waited orderly at the table in rich apparell, the pages arayed in silke robes, did fill great gemmes and pearles made in forme of Cups, with excellent wine. Then one brought in Candles and torches, and when we were sat downe and placed in order we began to talke, to laugh, and to be merry. And Byrrhena spake unto me and sayd, I pray you, Cousine, how like you our countrey? Verily I thinke there is no other City which hath like Temples, Baynes, and other commodities, which we have here. Further we have abundance of household stuffe, we have pleasure, we have ease, and when the Roman merchants arrive in this City they are gently and quietly entertained. . . .' An idle tale of a distant place and a long time ago, when the wolves were howling in the deep forests of these Midlands. There are no wolves now, only trams, which still go groaning to their sheds long after a Commercial's light has been extinguished.

RESIDENTIAL

A T FIRST it seemed hard luck that our house should not be ready for us. After such a magnificent return to town, what an anti-climax to spend a week or two in an hotel! But now I cannot help thinking that this, after all, is the best approach. With a fortress of domesticity at our backs, we should have begun our life here by merely making raids on Vanity Fair, by rushing out, grabbing a bit of experience and then hurrying back home with it. As it is, we have no home. I see these days at the hotel as a kind of little gateway, a darkish place, overhung with foliage, where you may stand for a moment and catch a glimpse of the mad gala of life in town. The curtain is trembling and all its folds are brightening, but first there is a brief prelude for muted strings and muffled horns. Our stay here is the prelude. With a place of our own we should not have felt the same queer glow of anticipation. Besides, we should have been too real. Now, it is London that is real and we are shadowy; and that, I maintain, is a good way to begin all over again.

This is a residential hotel. You realize that at once when you talk to the manageress. Every profession or trade has its great phrase that comes so roundly and comfortingly to the speaker's tongue. In the world of the theatre, for example, managers and others bring out their great phrase when they say they have Played To Capacity, and vaudeville artistes produce theirs when they announce that their act was so well received that it Stopped The Show. Ten minutes' conversation with the manageress of this hotel left me in no doubt as to what the great phrase is in residential hotel circles; it arrived time after time, always in triumph and capital letters: Booked Right Through The Winter. If manageresses of residential hotels ever hold a conference, I imagine that the hall will be decorated by a banner on which will be emblazoned in letters of crimson and gold— Booked Right Through The Winter. Spring, summer, autumn—what are these? Nothing; a few dreamy weeks of leaf and cloud; seasons so vague, so attenuated, that even the most opulent retired tea-planter, in search of a permanent south bedroom and corner table in the dining-room, could not book right through them. But Winter—that grand bulk of weeks and months—ah, what a thick, heavy, solid season!—and how delightful to see good guests, quiet maiden ladies and jolly grey-haired bachelors, all with suitcases stuffed with preference shares, booking right through, spiring their way from October to April!

It follows that we ourselves are nothing here. Surrounded as we are by people who have Booked Right Through The Winter or may do so at any moment, we are mere outlines of human beings. Our beds must be made and our rooms tidied; food must be placed before us; but on our forms and faces is not that steady light of B.R.T.T.W.: we are ghosts. And we feel like ghosts. Everything in the hotel conspires to rob us of any lingering traces of substantial humanity. I have no desire to complain of the place, which is, I have no doubt, one of the best residential hotels in town. It is clean and comfortable. In place of the usual ironmonger's assistant or retired cloakroom attendant, a chef is employed in the kitchen. The lighting arrangements are such that you can read in bed and see your face in the mirror. There are three large public rooms, and they have an adequate supply of armchairs, card tables, ash trays, to say nothing of wireless sets and the grand piano, the gramophone, and the ping-pong table. What more could a guest, even a B.R.T.T.W., require?

Strange as it may appear, however, I must confess that I for one cannot sit in any of these rooms for more than ten minutes. They are rooms that demand proudly to be thoroughly inspected when you are first looking over the hotel, but once you are a guest they do not ask you to sit in them. Indeed, they contrive to resent your presence. You can sit on the edge of one of their huge armchairs, waiting for somebody, but that is all. If you try to settle down, you find after five minutes or so that you are so uneasy you are compelled to get up and walk about or try another room. The walls, the carpets, the empty chairs, these things stare at you, ask one another what you are doing there, and finally tell you to go. You feel as if you had sneaked into the window of a furniture shop and were sitting in one of the chairs there. I have yet to see a card on one of the card tables, and the only time I left a little ash in one of the ash trays I hurried out the moment afterwards, like a man who had just committed sacrilege.

Sometimes there are people in these three public rooms. In the smoking-room, which has as much chill leather in it as any club in London, I have seen three men talking in a corner. I have caught them there three times now, and each time they appeared to be talking about laundry shares. What a staggering creative artist there must be behind reality! If you and I had to find a topic for three men in a corner of a smoking-room, we might rack our brains for six months and then not light on one so strange. Shares, or laundries—yes; but not laundry shares. In the drawing-room, I once caught two dim middle-aged women sitting very close together and whispering, and on another occasion I found a young girl there, standing in front of the piano and idly picking out a tune with one or two fingers. She was obviously not a guest at the hotel, not of British birth and parentage, and very reckless. It is the foreigners who grapple with these rooms. I have actually seen two Germans playing ping-pong in the third room, and making nearly as much noise as they did in the dining-room. And last Sunday I heard an incredible din in this ping-pong chamber and discovered that it was being made by a party of about fifteen members of some Latin race. They had put two tables together and were apparently holding a family conference round them. They ranged from a little old gentleman, who looked like a gnome pretending to be an Italian Senator, to various lemon-coloured chits in their early teens. They were all talking at once and they were all enjoying themselves. The Latin races must be curiously insensitive to atmosphere, though possibly three generations and fifteen of you are able to create an atmosphere of your own.

Perhaps if there were fifteen of us, we could do something; but there are not, and we are ghosts. I have heard myself referred to, by members of the staff here, as 'Number Twenty-Three,' and it never occurred to me to resent it. I feel like Number Twenty-Three. I have no possessions beyond a suitcase of clothes and a little shelf of brushes, razors, and the like. I have no place of my own, for you cannot call a bedroom such a place. I am surrounded by people whose names and histories I do not know, just as if I were at the theatre or sitting in a bus. The waitress who brings me my food is pleasant and attentive, but if I were to drop dead in the street to-morrow she would not care a rap and within a day or so would be putting a slice of turbot or a cutlet in front of another Twenty-Three. The chambermaid only knows me as so much luggage and litter, a little different from the luggage and litter of the last Twenty-Three. The porter sees me as a possible five bob. The manageress hardly sees me at all, for what am I, with my mere fortnight or so, but a midge compared with the giant creatures who have booked Right Through The Winter? And how many of these creatures are there in all the residential hotels of London?

I think about them and am lost in a sad wonder. What epics of personal history have dwindled into breakfast, lunch, tea, dinner, bed, a south room, a corner table, in these places! You make your little pile or come into your own or win through, do something final and heroic, and then you find yourself a perpetual guest, honoured no doubt in the office, respected by the servants, but leading a spectral life. Nobody wants to hear what a trial Aunt Hilda was before she finally died and left you all her money. Nobody wants to hear your stories of India or Burma or China. How easy it must be to die in these places!——just a matter of not getting up one morning, of slipping away and booking right through a million winters.

AT A DANCE

IT WAS a private dance, chiefly intended for girls and boys in their late 'teens and early 'twenties, but a few 'old 'uns,' friends of the family, were thrown in, and that is how I came to be there. I have not been to a dance of this kind for years and years. I am not a dancing man. When I was a boy I learned to go through all the old dances, waltz, two step, lancers, in a rough and ready fashion, and now and again I went to dances, hot and abashed, and did what I could. Then I forgot about dancing. The war came, the war went, and everybody began dancing, but I never bothered to learn all the new dances. Recently, however, I have been compelled to dance a bit, chiefly because we happen to have a drawing-room with a slippery parquet floor, and a gramophone. Every woman under forty who comes to this house insists upon showing me how to dance. Unfortunately they all seem to have different methods themselves, so that I never make any progress. I think my greatest weakness is that I am not fierce enough. Some-times they undertake to show me what a competent male is expected to do in this dancing, and then I find myself very firmly grasped and yanked round the room in a most astonishing manner. 'There!' they gasp. 'Thank you!' I gasp back at them. But I never find I can do it myself. The fact is—to be quite candid—I cannot escape from the feeling that it is all rather indelicate. I am too shy to handle a succession of strange women in this fashion. No doubt if I were filled up with liquor and then loosed among the girls of Shanghai or San Francisco, or some other remote place, I could act the part of a real he-man dancer tolerably well.

The result is that now, in the dancing world, I am neither fish nor flesh. 'I don't *really*,' I reply. 'I'm the worst dancer in the world.' They take this for modesty (though why they should I cannot imagine, for I give no indication in other matters that I am afflicted by modesty) and insist upon my dancing. Then they learn that I was speaking the truth. A girl at the dance the other night did not believe me when I told her how bad I was, but after we had struggled and bumped round the room a few times, I watched the discovery of my solid veracity—one of my most marked traits—dawning hideously upon her. I noticed her once or twice later in the evening, secure in the arms of graceful and dashing youths, and there was then a look of seraphic bliss on her face. Probably she would never have realized what bliss there was on these heights if it had not been for me. But I steadfastly refused to have anything to do with such girls again during the dance, and when I was pressed into service—which happened about once every half-hour or so—I contrived to find partners among nice, jolly incompetent women of my own age, who regarded a bumping progress round the room as a bit of a lark—bless them! Not for me those solemn young high priestesses of the cult.

And how solemn they are, the dancing youngsters! When I arrived, the dance could not have been going on for more than about a quarter of an hour, and the very first thing that surprised me was the fact that they were all *at it* even then, and indeed looked as if they had been dancing away for hours. There was something so curiously purposeful about these girls and boys. They had gone there to dance, and so they danced, probably beginning within two minutes of their arrival. Now in my time—and yours too, I suppose, for nobody under thirty ever reads anything I write—

we should never have dreamt of setting to work with such brisk efficiency. We chatted; we grinned in corners; we looked stealthily at the girls; we hung about; we waited for inspiration. There was none of this nonsense about these bright young post-war beings. They were not people who 'did a bit of' dancing: they were dancers; and if they had been conscientious professionals, paid by the hour, they could not have danced oftener nor harder.

Most of them danced very well, too. Even I could see that. The youths, even the young boys, all danced seriously. They were clearly as anxious to be good dancers as they were to be good crick-eters or lawn-tennis players. Nothing, not even the most startling list of figures about dance-halls and cabarets and night clubs, could better illustrate the progress that dancing has made in the world than the attitude of those boys. Before the war the ordinary boy had no particular desire to dance, and would have regarded with contempt any other boy who took dancing seriously and tried to im-prove his steps just as he had tried to improve his batting and bowling. We were oafs in those days. I do not know, but nevertheless I am almost certain that very young men and boys these days have a genuine admiration for the fellows who dance better than themselves. There was nothing oafish about the youths I saw the other night. On the other hand, there was no suggestion of gaiety, high spirits. They were enjoying themselves—that was obvious—but they were not in heaven for an hour or two. No, they were simply serious practitioners. If they felt there was anything glamorous about the occasion, they were successful in hiding any trace of the feeling. They were there, on solid ground, on this earth, having a good night's dancing. I do not think we were ever like that. I fancy we used to waver on these occasions between misery and joy, never touched solid ground, but shot from hell to heaven. At one minute a dance was all a stupid business and we cursed ourselves for consenting to go. At the next minute—though it was a rare next minute—the whole thing was transformed by some sudden intoxication in the blood, and had all the glamour of a happy dream. Perhaps there is here all the difference between two generations, two worlds—with a crumbling trench between them.

I noticed a further difference. When I was in my late teens, girls liked dancing and boys did not, but nevertheless, at the actual dances, the girls—

or at least, those with any pretensions to good looks—queened it over us. We always felt that it was a vast piece of condescension on their part to dance with us at all. We were honoured by their notice. A smile or two—and we began to lose our heads. All that has gone. Now, it seems to me, the boys have the upper hand. It is they who are courted by the girls. If, at their age, I had had so many pretty eager creatures sighing for a dance with me, I do not know what would have happened to me, so completely would my head have been turned. But these youths of to-day accept these attentions from the other sex with a cool complacency that is almost godlike. It is only— their attitude declares—what a fellow must expect, and of course one must have girls to dance with.

The most godlike of all the young gentlemen at the dance, the other night, was one I found myself calling The Olympian. He was up at Ox-ford—and at the most Olympian college—and might have been twenty or twenty-one. His hair was thick and fair, his eyes bright and impudent, and his dancing—well, I do not really know what his dancing was, except that it was the kind that all the young girls there obviously preferred.

They adored him. You could see them brightening at his approach and fading out again when he had passed them. I must do him the justice to observe that, unlike most gods, he appeared to distribute his favours impartially. It is terrible to think that he had the power to wreck a friendship (begun in the fourth form, and wonderfully carried on right through the sixth, and out at the other end) with a nod and a smile. So strong was the atmosphere of adoration that had been created all round him that I began to be affected by it a little myself; and I honestly believe I should have been flattered if The Olympian had spoken to me. The last time I saw him he was in the hall, and about three girls were imploring him to stay a little longer and dance with them or their friends. But no, he had to look in at some other dance, and off he went, with a captivating little swagger, followed by an admiring friend, into the night, where (though he does not know it yet) there are waiting such things as mortgages, bank managers, income-tax officials, wrinkles, baldness, a paunch, hardening of the arteries, the twilight of the gods. And I say this sadly, and without the malicious satisfaction born of envy.

But before I went I caught sight of some of

those young people sitting on the stairs. I had not thought them capable of such a thing. All the evidence pointed to the stairs having been long forgotten as a sitting-out place. 'Why,' I told myself excitedly, 'they'll be falling in love next!' And I blessed them under my breath as I passed, out of that rich patriarchal store of kindly sentiment that properly belongs to a man born as long ago as in 1894.

JUST AFTER CHRISTMAS

As a matter of fact, this is not by J. B. Priestley at all, but by me, William Priestley. That is my name, as you would see for yourself if you took a look at my collar, a very handsome one, too, brass-studded. The reason why I am doing this instead of him (it is him, isn't it? I'm very rusty in my grammar) is because he doesn't want to do it at all this week and told me so, as he sat yawning in a chair, and so I said I would do it for him. He said he didn't care who did it so long as he didn't, and that if I had a subject I could go ahead. No thanks of any kind—just that.

This is the kind of thing a dog has to put up with, even an aristocratic Sealyham like me. I don't want to be snobbish—and nobody could say I'm a snobbish dog; in fact, I'm always getting into trouble because I don't mind passing the time of the day with a dog of any class when I'm out for a walk—but there's nobody here can show such a pedigree as I have, prizes and prizes on both sides of the family. Suppose there had been Man shows, how many prizes would my master and mistress's parents and aunts and uncles and grandfathers and grandmothers have got? Not so many. Probably none. However, thanks or no thanks, I promised to write this for him and I like to keep my bark. I told him I had a subject, but that wasn't strictly true. I haven't any particular subject, but I thought that as this is my first (and probably last) appearance, nobody would mind if I just barked about things in general.

I've no intention of doing this sort of thing often, I can tell you. Once in a long while is quite enough for me. I'm a thoroughly doggy dog and I like notice and applause as much as the next dog, but I draw the line at authorship. A trick now and again to get a pat or two is all very well, but to be doing it all day and then perhaps to get nothing much—no, not for me. And to have to pretend (is that all right? It looks queer) you don't care! I know. There are men—authors— who come here and sit in the study upstairs with my master, and sometimes, if I've nothing better to do, I look in and listen to them talking. You never heard such stuff! 'Well, old man,' they say, 'I don't care a rap what the reviewers say. I never look at reviews.' And then: 'I don't mind about the book not selling. Never thought it would.

But I must say, when I see rubbish like So-and-so's latest, it makes me ——!' And here's another favourite—I must have heard it dozens of times: 'The fact is, old man, I shall have to change my publisher. That's the real trouble. Thingumbobs *won't* advertise. How can they expect people to buy a book when they don't advertise it? I've a jolly good mind to go to Bobumthings. Now they *do* know how to put a book over. Look at the way they've sold that thing of Bunkum's.' It's the same old stuff every time. And all pretence. My master's as bad as the rest. They're all alike, these authors. You don't catch me becoming one.

A lot of dogs are going in for writing these days, though. And some of them are making a good thing out of it. Somebody told me the other day that that Pekinese who writes 'From My Basket in Mayfair' is getting five cutlets and three jugs of cream for every article. And I know for a fact that the Irish Setter who does 'A Londoner's Dog' is paid at the rate of ten bones a thousand words. Those are the journalists, of course, and most of the dogs who write books don't make as much as that. But they seem to do pretty well. There's an old pug down the road who is always writing reminiscences, 'Ten Years with a Dowager,' 'Bishops and Butlers I Have Known,' and so on, and I believe she makes quite respectable bonery out of it. This is a very literary neighbourhood, of course. I hardly ever take a walk without smelling several dogs who are authors. A fox terrier who lives in the next street has taken to writing detective tales—it was he who wrote 'The Hambone Mystery' and 'Towser's Last Case'— and they tell me he is burying bones now as fast as he can. And the chow at No. 53 is a poet, or at any rate a sort of poet, for I must say I don't much care for this modern free verse stuff he goes in for. Here is a thing of his he showed me the other day:

> Biscuits athwart
>   And impermanently poised
> Trust.
>   Hollow engines
>   Motionless.
> Paid for.
>   Come lady, it scabrously falls,
>   So let us
> Feast, feast, feast Egyptians.

He told me it took him four weeks to work that out, and I replied that made it all the worse. And so it does, don't you think? His mistress at No.

53 is a rich American woman, and I think that explains a good deal.

But I don't think I have explained exactly why I come to be doing this. The fact is, my master, like everybody in this house except me, has eaten too much this week. Dogs are supposed to be very fond of eating, and I admit I enjoy a good meal, but really there's hardly a single dog of my acquaintance who isn't disgusted at the way humans go on. I have one meal a day, that's all. There are times during the morning when I have no objection to a mere snack, a biscuit or something of that kind, but I don't want more than that. But the people here—the little ones as well as the big ones—hardly ever stop eating. And this week has been terrible. It's been a queer week altogether. The little ones have been jumping about making more noise than usual—not that I mind that; I like a romp with them, so long as there is no tail-pulling and other hooliganism—and the whole house has been full of people and brown paper and string and prickly green stuff. And everybody has been saying something about 'Erry Issmus'. All sorts of strangers actually came to the front door, saying 'Erry Issmus' or whatever it is, until I had a sore throat, barking at them to go away. But it is the eating that has really sickened me. I am ready to make as many allowances as the next dog for humans, but there is a limit. I could understand it if it were only the little ones, but my master has been one of the worst. It seems he is very fond of some stuff—you never smelt anything more sickly—called pudding, and some other stuff called 'minspy,' and he has gobbled so much of these things that now he can do nothing but sit in a chair and yawn and yawn, a horrible sight. He is getting quite fat, but he says he doesn't care, though I think he does.

He keeps all the things he writes in a kind of red box, and the other day they were all lying on the floor and I had a glance through them. And I was surprised, I can tell you. There's so much pretence about it. Now, I don't fancy myself as an author or journalist or anything of that kind, and when I do write it is very rough-and-ready stuff I turn out, I know, but it is honest and sincere. I'm not pretending to be anyone else but William Priestley, the Sealyham at 27 Well Walk, Hampstead. I write—so to bark—to my collar. But my master is a complete fraud. To begin with, I notice that he pretends to be one of those quiet, kind, wise, elderly men, who go about and notice everything without saying much. At least, that is the sort of man I should imagine him to be if I did not know him but only read these things he writes. And he is not a bit like that, really. He is not very old, and would look quite young if he ate and drank less and took more exercise—as I am always suggesting to him. He is neither quiet nor wise, but a rather loud-voiced, bullying sort of man who can be quite as silly—sillier even— than any of the little ones here. And then he hardly ever goes anywhere, and when he does he never notices anything, as I have heard my mistress say more than once. He makes it all up at home, sitting in the study blowing that horrible smoke out of his mouth. And he has a tremendous sense of his own importance, all based on nothing much, except of course that he *is* my master and there are not many men in Hampstead who have a first-class Sealyham to wag a tail at them every time they come in—and to write their essays for them.

He says: 'Just wish them a Happy New Year, William, and then chuck it.' So that's all. Good-bye—wuff, wuff!

WHAT a misery they are, these colds in the head! I had begun to think that I was becoming immune from them, when one descended upon me early last week. Where it came from, I do not know. I had been leading my ordinary life and do not remember having wet feet or sitting in a draught or anything of that kind. There appeared to be no reason why the thing should visit me, and I believe there was no reason outside the malice of the little gods who are for ever playing tricks with our lives. I believe, too, that the doctors who tell us why we have these visitations are merely bluffing. Some of them, I know, will say that it is because we do not go out enough, because we need fresh air. But I had colds in the head when I was in the army and worked, played, slept, ate and drank in the open air. I am convinced that these things cannot be explained by the amount of fresh air we have, nor by wet feet nor draughts nor even microbes. They come from the malicious little gods, who remark that we are beginning to feel rather more at ease in the world and so decide to 'larn' us. One of them—a Polar deity with a vast icy hand is instructed to come down and creep into our bedrooms some time in the small hours, and once there he thrusts his monstrous index finger under the clothes and touches us on the small of the back. That is where he always touches me, and all the following day I can feel the place a nasty little patch of cold in my back. The rest of my body may be like a roasted apple, but that patch still remains cold, a fact that proves its supernatural origin. I wish Blake had thought of this as a subject for a drawing and had shown us that great icy hand moving towards the bed. Perhaps Blake never had colds in the head.

I had my little cold patch last Tuesday morning and by nightfall I was helpless in the grip of the thing. The next three days were simply a procession of handkerchiefs. On the first day, old and despised inhabitants of the handkerchief drawer, forgotten monstrosities with purple and green borders, presents from remote aunts, were called out for duty, but by the end of the third day, acres of fair linen, most delicately hemmed, had come and gone. All the time I felt rather hungry, but I could not enjoy my food. Tea tasted queer. I had to put aside my pipe, of course, because the tobacco had taken on a new and awful flavour of its own. Could there be anything more artfully malicious than this absurd complaint? You do not feel really ill, and because you are deprived of all manner of pleasures, you feel more than usually dependent on a pipe, but by some curious and diabolical contrivance you are also deprived of your pipe. I say that you do not feel ill, and neither do you, but that does not mean that you feel well. You merely feel something between the two—queer. It is this queerness that is so distasteful. With streaming eyes, a very red nose and a hoarse voice, you look like a low comedian, and the other people in the house, victims of a most childish association of ideas, would seem to imagine that really you are doing it all for fun, that you have decided to devote several days to the task of imitating Mr. Leslie Hènson or Mr. A. W. Bascomb. 'Well, you *have* got a cold!' they cry, and then they go off into peals of laughter. And, of course, by this time, your produdciashud turds every rebark you bake iddo a grade joag.

It would not be so bad if a cold in the head ever rose into the dignity of an illness. I think I would rather be downright ill. There is a touch of drama about being ill. You become the centre of interest; doctors are called in to see you; everybody tiptoes in and out of the room; you are a strange romantic figure. There is nothing of this with a cold in the head. No doctor suggests that you ought to drop everything and go to the Riviera or take a trip to Honolulu. No bulletins are issued to anxious friends. No delicately modulated voice beseeches you to try a little of this specially prepared jelly. No expensive fruits find their way to your bedside. You are simply the leading domestic joke of the week. Everybody knows exactly what is wrong with you, so that when people are not laughing at you, they are proposing infallible remedies. It is significant that all these remedies are grotesque and my own opinion is that they are devised simply to supply additional comic 'business' to the apparent farce. Everybody sees you as a comic figure, and so everybody tries to heighten the fun under pretence of curing you. Thus, it is suggested that you should sit with your feet in mustard-and-water, that you should have a poultice clapped on you, that you should put your face in a great steaming bowl, filled with some absurd preparation, and be covered with a towel so that you cannot breathe, that you should anoint

« 147 »

your nostrils with a poisonous-looking green substance. When I was younger, I would fall in with these suggestions with all the simplicity of Jourdain himself, and I have no doubt that I kept the house in a roar. Now I will have none of them. I test the sincerity of those who tell me that they wish to see me better by proposing to them that they should attempt to cure me in my own way. If they do not fall in with my own suggestion, then I dismiss them as mere stage-managers of farce. If they do agree, then I ask them to procure a quantity of sugar and lemon-juice, a kettle, a jug, and some whisky, rum, brandy, or gin.

I trust that these beneficent spirits will never be completely banished from the world, but if they are to be, then, in the name of Pity herself, let their banishment be postponed until the last cold in the head has gone. It is a shame that we should have to depend sometimes on the fumes of spirits for cheerfulness, but it is a greater shame that we should be cursed by these visitations of cold. They ruin you as a normal happy man and yet they will not allow you to find satisfaction in being an invalid. They leave you most malevolently in a barren midair. It is bad enough to be deprived of a palate, to look like a low comedian, to be compelled to dab away, day and night, with innumerable handkerchiefs, but that is not the worst. By some horrible hocus-pocus, they take away your very soul. Such, at least, is my experience. No sooner has one of these colds descended upon me than I become a different creature, one of an obviously lower order. It is as if I were the little boy in Hans Andersen's *Snow Queen*. I see everything differently. My feelings are all changed. Gone are those noble enthusiasms that leaven my poor clay. I care not a fig for the Good, the True, the Beautiful. Music is nothing but an irritating din or a wearisome buzz. I have lost all relish for poetry. If Keats offered me half a dozen new Odes as good as the *Nightingale* and the *Grecian Urn*, I would not thank him for them. Anything passionate or eloquent in literature becomes distasteful to me during these times. You could put before me the whole pageant of man's loves and dreams, and it would receive from me nothing but a sniff—that is, an extra sniff. I become 'a *qui bono* man.' I see my fellow mortals as cunning or idiotic animals, so many foxes and geese. I sniff away their visions, heroisms, sacrifices, even their good intentions. With one sweep of my germ-laden handkerchief, I banish all the noble and gay and passionate things from this world. That is the sort of person I am when I have a cold in the head. There are other people too, I have noticed, who are like that. Some people must have colds in their heads all the time.

I enjoy my soul, just as I enjoy my pipe, all the more when my cold finally takes its leave. But it is humiliating to have a soul that appears to be at the mercy of a tiny patch of cold in the back. It makes me angry to think that a little visitation of this kind can turn me into an entirely different creature. If my appreciation of Beethoven's late spring quartets and Turner's water-colours and Keats's Odes and Meredith's account of Richard Feverel and his Lucy meeting by the river, if my appreciation of these and other lovely things depends upon the number of handkerchiefs I use during the day, then where are we? If, every time I put away my pipe for a few days, I have also to put away the Good, the True, the Beautiful, what sort of a world is this? If I assume another personality with my thick dressing-gown, who on earth am I? These are disturbing queries, I fancy, but they suit my humour. I am now in the last stages of the cold, the thick stage, and I have said good-bye to the procession of handkerchiefs and have got a glimpse of my returning soul. I am doing very well, but ab dod quide bedder yed.

ALMOST every night for the last few weeks I have taken a little holiday. When I have gone to bed I have also gone to Barsetshire. There are a good many actual counties about which I know less than I do about this Barset. Huntingdon, Bedford and Hereford are not so real to me. How could they be? I do not visit them every night just before I go to sleep and am hardly ever told what is going on there. But I know what is happening in Barset. Let me give you the news. Mr. Harding has left Hiram's Hospital; Proudie is Bishop and Arabin is now Dean; Mary Thorne has come into a fortune and married Frank Gresham; Lucy Robartes is now Lady Lufton and very handsome she looks; Lily Dale has refused Johnny Eames, who is doing so well up in London; poor Mr. Crawley has been accused of stealing a cheque for twenty pounds and Archdeacon Grantly is worried about the Plumstead foxes.

So you see—if you are sensible enough to be a fellow student of Trollope—that I am now deep in the *Last Chronicle* again, and that Mrs. Proudie is about to be killed off at any moment. If Trollope had not overheard that fellow at his club declaring that he was sick and tired of Mrs. Proudie, he would never have killed her off as he did, and we might have had half a dozen more stories of Barset and all the folk we have come to know so well. Confound that wretched clubman! Mrs. Proudie was worth ten of him. Why couldn't somebody have killed *him* off? If he didn't like to read about Mrs. Proudie, there was nothing to prevent him from leaving Trollope alone. People overlook this little fact when they take up such a hoity-toity attitude towards books. There is no law compelling you to read books you dislike, so why not pass on to what you do like, without making a fuss? I trust there is some bookless inferno set apart for these spoilers and interrupters of literature, for 'persons from Porlock' and clubmen who are bored by Mrs. Proudie.

Barset is a capital place to end the day in because it is so different from the rest of the world we know. It is indeed a haven of rest. True, there are many things not found there that are good in themselves. Thus there is no poetry in Barset; no light that never was on land or sea; no golden romantic haze, such as you may discover, any early morning in spring, transfiguring the meadows and streams near Richard Feverel's home. Barset is a place without *atmosphere*. Sun, moon, and stars there are merely astronomical terms. If you tried to tell the people of Barchester about Moby Dick, they would have you locked up. I was about to say that Don Quixote would have been given only half an hour in which to leave the city, but then I remember our old friend, Mr. Harding, who, I will swear, would have taken Don Quixote under his roof and, no doubt, would have played the 'cello to him.

Just as there is no poetry, so too there are no high spirits, none of those colossal absurdities that are so much larger than life that they are really political, being evidences not of what life is but of what it ought to be. Mr. Micawber can find his way to Canterbury, but you may be sure that he could never find his way to Barchester, which has neither corn nor coals for him; there is no clerkship awaiting Dick Swiveller there, and no nursing, either by day or night, that could possibly fall into the grasp of Mrs. Gamp. I do not mean to say that there is no fun, for there is plenty of that—think of the Stanhopes (who might have come straight out of the Chelsea fiction of our time) at the Proudies' party—but there is certainly no enchanting idiocy, there are no divinely daft characters. These can only exist in a rich atmosphere, full of haze and sudden gleams from some far-away strange sun.

On the other hand, though, there are no nerves, no obsessions, no unconscious minds, in Barset. (Mr. Crawley, who seems to have stalked in from another world, is the exception.) It is a great relief to spend some time in the company of characters who know what they are doing, who have set their minds on marrying the prettiest girl in the village, or on having five hundred a year, and do not drearily chatter their lives away. That the county has very few ideas, I will freely confess. Though the foreground is black with clergymen, there is precious little religion in Barset. Mr. Crawley is the only one who continually bothers about God, and he is obviously an odd fish and only escapes not being a gentleman by the skin of his teeth. And although we hear a certain amount of talk about politics and even assist at an election or two, the politics are not very real, merely a matter of being for or against the Duke of Omnium, of red posters and blue posters.

Music and pictures and books are mentioned

too, but it is obvious that nobody in Barset really cares a fig about art. A man who talked aesthetics there would soon find himself dining at home every night. No, Barset does not trouble itself with any concern for ideas. It is a place crammed with real things, such as puddings and mortgages and horses and marriage settlements and port. That is one reason—I feel it is an act of treachery even to whisper it, but the truth must be told— why the evenings are so dull here. You must have noticed that. Every one begins to yawn about half-past nine. Once the children have been seen to bed, the horses stabled, the dinner eaten and the de-canter handed round, there is nothing more to do. That is why Mrs. Proudie is such a godsend to the place. She put a stop to the whist that old Bishop Grantly introduced into the Palace itself, but she set going all manner of intrigues that stirred everybody up and made it possible to keep an evening going fairly briskly until half-past ten. She hurled topics for excited talk into the county like bricks into a dull pool. I do not like to think what Barset must have been like between stories, as it were, after the marriage had been made or the preferment, when everybody was supposed to be living happily ever after: it must have been incredibly dull, all perfunctory sermons, puddings and yawns.

That does not matter, however, because we only find our way there when something is happening, not enough to leave us gasping or heart-sick but just enough to make us travel happily from Barchester to Allington, Greshambury to Hogglestock, in quest of the latest news. There is a fine balance between excitement and a sense of solid comfort. We feel as if we were spending a week or two with pleasant old friends and had found that they had got up a little scandal or intrigue just to help us to pass the long mornings and evenings. I know no fiction that suggests better than this a comfortable restful holiday. That does not mean that I would like my contemporaries to be Trollopes. If they gave us such a world as we find in Barset, they would be merely faking, making an absurd pretence that a middle-aged Queen Victoria was still on the throne. We are, it seems, all nerves and baffled aspirations, whirling in ideas and drifting in conduct, always talking and thinking about love and finding no place of rest in it, members of a social order that is like a kaleidoscope, so free to do what we please that we do nothing but wonder what is worth doing, so far removed from the people who shaped their lives under certain fixed conditions that we are never sure whether we are lords of destiny or mere gnats in the hour's sunshine; and our novelists must write about us as they find us. In theory, it is such times as these, when everybody is so free, so crammed with ideas, so ready to talk about anything or make any experiment in conduct, that ought to produce the most exciting and gorgeous novels.

But I am beginning to doubt whether actual practice is bearing out the theory. Those people in Barset, so comfortable, so dull, so limited in their ideas, so rigidly fixed in their social life, are better people to read about than those clever fellows and bold girls who drift from studio to night-club, from Oxford to Florence, in the novels that pile up on our tables. 'Very clever, very sensitive, prettily done,' we murmur after having read a few chapters or so, but we have no objection to leaving these people to chatter away in their own company, and some of us hurry away to Paddington and take the train again to Barchester, to secure a place at the dinner-table of Thorne of Ullathorne or to peep into poor Bishop Proudie's study.

Sir Walter Raleigh, who was always hitting

nails on the head, banged one of them most happily when he remarked in a letter: 'I lay in bed this morning for a little and read Trollope. I'm afraid it's no good anyone telling me that Thackeray is a better novelist than Trollope. . . . Trollope starts off with an ordinary people, that bore you in life and in books, and makes an epic of them because he understands affection, which the others take for granted or are superior about. I wish there were a Trollope movement, it would be so healthy.' There—as the preachers used to say—is a thought for the week. In how many recent and much talked of novels is there even a glint of affection? The only thing that puzzles me in this passage of Raleigh's is his lying in bed *in the morning* reading Trollope. Evening, I am sure, is the proper time, so that you can have a pleasant rendezvous with Sleep in the close at Barchester.

Not long ago, in one of our Law Courts, a gentleman declared that he had spent ten years on a bibliography of Oscar Wilde. The case in which this gentleman figured was rather an amusing one, and judge and counsel did not hesitate to join in the fun, so that a good deal of laughter was reported. But no laughter followed this reference to the ten years' task. It would seem to have been made solemnly, perhaps just seasoned with the scholar's grave pride, and to have been received in the same spirit. After all it is something to have spent ten years on a single task, for these are the days of snappy and patchy jobs, when every one seems to want a piece of work to be like the inevitable cigarette that accompanies the performance of it, a few puffs and nothing more. Perhaps a hush of awe fell on the assembled court when these ten years of dedicated toil were mentioned. No matter how we may praise idleness, we can never escape being impressed by a sustained piece of work. Yet there is something very fantastic about this piece of work, and, with all respect to the gentleman who was so long engaged with it, I cannot help thinking that I should have laughed if I had been in the court. And surely Wilde himself would have laughed if he had been there. How trifling were his own labours beside those of his bibliographers! You would have to subtract a great deal from ten years before you arrived at the amount of time that Wilde spent writing the works so lovingly catalogued. Except in talk, he was incorrigibly indolent, and it is perhaps the supreme paradox of this paradoxical creature's life that while he pretended to sacrifice everything for art, he really sacrificed nothing at all, not even a little time. His style is a most amusing fake, if only because it smells of the lamp and yet has never had a lamp near it, being in reality the kind of style that can be prattled away without any trouble. He spent his time declaring that nothing in this life mattered but taste and the artistic conscience, and nearly all his work is ruined by the obvious absence of both in the man who hastily and carelessly penned it between bouts of talk.

His admiring bibliographers would seem to have restored the balance by being incredibly diligent, by laboriously collecting and cataloguing every trifle he ever wrote. These people seem to me as fantastic as creatures from the moon. I cannot understand their point of view. If they work merely because they are paid to do it, then their motive is comprehensible, and I simply transfer my amazement to the persons who summon them to such labours. These persons, I take it, are bibliophiles, and I have long been mystified by the bibliophiles. I suppose that I have bought, borrowed, stolen, and ultimately read as many books as most men of my age; I have written some books, and I have assisted, if only very humbly, in the publication of a great many more; so that when books are in question, I feel on fairly safe ground. But when books become *biblia*, I am utterly lost. The bibliographer, so gravely proud of his dates and title-pages, so triumphant when, after years of inquiry, he produces some scrap of writing or other that his author probably wished off the face of the earth, I can vaguely respect him because he is at once passionately industrious and selfless, but he seems as strange as an alchemist. And his patrons, the bibliophiles, appear to be people utterly remote from the honest bookmen of my acquaintance. Some of them, of course, are not interested in literature, do not regard a book merely as a vehicle of the spirit but as something to be collected, a substitute for Roman coins or old English teapots. It is difficult to understand how such people contrive to remain uninterested in the content of the books they acquire; but it is not they who really puzzle me. It is that far larger class of dainty deckle-edged and hand-made-paper readers, for whom the catalogues of Rare Books and Modern First Editions are produced, which mystifies me. I cannot grasp their point of view.

These catalogues arrive here every week, probably because I occasionally spend a few shillings on a book that is out of print. Some of them are not very puzzling because they obviously appeal to a certain marked taste. Many of their items are labelled 'curious.' Such catalogues are apparently convenient because they enable a man who has a taste for the indecent to pretend to himself that he is merely interested in fine literature. But why be so canting and hypocritical? I cannot understand these people who must have their dirty stories exquisitely printed on hand-made paper and bound in buckram, who want their indecency carefully arranged in their library, who solace themselves with it far from the companionship and honest laughter of the smoking-room and the bar. Matter of this kind, I should have thought, would not survive such a cold-blooded approach, and I have a suspicion that if I met these queer patrons of fine literature I should not like them. Nor do their booksellers, with their sniggering 'curious,' inspire me with any confidence as fellow citizens. I suspect that they are the rich relations of those creatures who keep grimy and furtive little shops filled with dreary trash from the French and horribly labelled pills for debilitated men.

Most of the catalogues I receive, however, do not belong to this class, and would seem to be honestly concerned with literature. But their concern cannot be referred to any explicable standard of judgment. Thus, the Modern First Edition business either rests on a chaos of literary taste, or is based on canons outside my comprehension. I cannot understand why the books of some people should be apparently so valuable, and the books of other people, not inferior as writers and perhaps demonstrably superior, should be worth little or nothing. I have no personal feeling on the matter. I have seen my own books marked above their published price (though not much above) in these lists, and I have also seen the very same editions of the very same books marked below their published price ('nice copy,' too) in these lists. Who are these critics of literature who decide that Smith's *Youth in Chains*, nice copy of the first edition with dropped letter on title-page, shall be worth £2 10s., and that Brown's *The Freedom of Age*, first edition in original jacket, shall be worth 2s. 9d.? Why do these mysterious bibliophiles put Smith so high and Brown so low? I have before me, as I write, one of these catalogues of first editions of contemporary authors. It is possible that I am a little chagrined at discovering that certain books I reviewed briefly a few years ago and then gave away or sold for half a crown are now fetching pounds. But the values suggest a most fantastic taste in literature. A foreigner who imagined that these prices represented the real standing of the authors concerned would have the most grotesque notion of our literary taste. He would come to the conclusion that our ideal of a book would be a few early and over-written essays by Mr. Max Beerbohm with a frontispiece by Aubrey Beardsley and a misprint on the title-page.

There is, too, in this catalogue, which is a large and most sumptuous affair, a very solemn *Bibliography of the First Editions* of a certain young novelist. I have not a word to say, in this place or in any other, against this young novelist, but for the life of me I cannot understand why anyone should have gone to the trouble of noting all the details of his books, size and binding and number of pages, and all the rest of it. The next step will be to issue a bibliography for collectors of those writers who have not yet published a book but have had a manuscript accepted by the publishers, who will furnish particulars of the binding and the number of pages. It would seem that while the bookmen grow less, the bibliophiles increase and call for more and more grotesque antics.

AT THE VERDUN FILM

IT WAS very kind of the Gaumont Company
to invite me to the Marble Arch Pavilion to
see the great film *Verdun*. I don't know why they
did it. Most of the other guests seemed to be
political and military men. (And the number of
military bigwigs who look like first cousins of
Alice's White Knight is surprising.) There were
hardly any literary gents there, though I did catch
sight of one famous novelist. I will not tell you
his name; I will only say that I kept wondering
what he thought about this tragic shadow show,
whether it was inducing in him first-class sensations or merely second-class sensations, and how
his human machine was running that night. I also
caught a glimpse of the pale and handsome face of
Sir Philip Gibbs, and thought it was very clever
of the management to have him there, for where
there is a war—and there is a war in *Verdun*—
there must be Sir Philip Gibbs. Altogether it
was a very curious evening, and I am grateful to
the film company for having presented me with it.

The evening began like a party. The Marble

Arch Pavilion was at home to you; it was dressed up; you were dressed up; and from 8.15 to 8.30 you bobbed and smiled at one another. Everybody looked about to see if friends were present, and if they were present then there was a lot of Excuse Me's and crossing over and How D'You Do's and handshakings. At the end of the evening the party atmosphere was intensified. We were all very festive indeed, at the expense of the film company. We ate sandwiches, nibbled *petit fours*, accepted large cigars, and floated happily on a tide of *Pol Roger* 1916. The military gentlemen unbent and looked as if they were letting out a number of those secrets that have been public property since 1918. The youngish women (I suspected that they were concocters of gossip paragraphs for the penny papers) who had stalked in so fiercely earlier in the evening now looked very gay indeed, and behaved as if they were amiable cockatoos. Gentlemen connected with the management, gentlemen with the broadest of smiles above their white ties, walked from group to group, *Pol Roger* in hand, and gave the impression that it was everybody's birthday.

I myself was very happy, chiefly because I had discovered the identity of a certain member of the company, a ruddy, handsome, rather distinguished looking man. For ten minutes I puzzled my head about him, knowing very well that I had met him somewhere, and I should have gone home miserable if I had not suddenly recollected that he had once brought me tea at the Haymarket Stores, and was indeed their ruddiest and most handsome waiter. It was a very jolly party. What a life these film critics must have if every big picture is launched on such golden tides of champagne and wreathed about with such smoke of Havana! If this is the way an austere war film is introduced, what happens when a picture of a girl's life in the cabarets of New York is brought over here? This is something they never mention in their solemn film notes. They might at least give us poor outsiders a hint of the brands employed, thus: 'The latest night life comedy, *Naughty Sadie* (Bollinger 1912 and Corona Corona) was shown privately yesterday.' When these fellows think of reviewers, dusty, thirsty, compelled to buy and smoke an inferior Navy Cut, they must chuckle.

What was so odd, however, about last Monday night was the contrast between the beginning and end of the evening and what happened between. When we had nodded and smiled and settled in

our seats, the lights went out and we found ourselves back again in the War, the War with the
capital letter, the real one. *Verdun* is a masterpiece. It is the work of a man and an artist. It
does not show you the military and amorous
antics of a crowd of actors, actresses and dressed-up
supers, assisted by a few men from the local fire-
work factory; it shows you the War. It has been
conceived in no narrow and catchpenny spirit of
nationalism—the Germans are as sympathetically
treated as the French and English—and it has
been carried out with real imagination and amazing skill. The difference between *Verdun* and the
average American war film, such as *The Big
Parade*, is the difference between the Eroica and
'Over There' or 'Keep the Home Fires Burning.'
The success enjoyed by *The Big Parade* was a dis-
grace to the English public, who ought to have
had more sense. That film may have dealt with
a war, but if it did it was some war between Hol-
lywood and some other conglomeration of film
studios. It was a war of actors. You saw actors
marching, actors resting in billets and indulging in
comic relief, actors making love to a pretty film
star, actors being rushed to the front in theatrical

lorries, actors being killed by property shell-fire. It was obviously an army rationed with hair-oil, sticks of grease paint, and press-cuttings.

There are no actors in *Verdun*, at least you never think of its personages as actors. The soldiers and peasants look and act like soldiers and peasants. The shell-fire and machine-gunning are the real thing. If you are curious about such matters you can read an account of the immense pains taken by the producer, but it is not necessary you should, for the film itself is there. The one objection I have to the film—apart from a few lapses into sentimentality of the French kind, which is even more bludgeoning than ours—is that, being a genuine work of art, it has a dangerous tragic beauty. I thought at first that here was a film that would knock the belligerent nonsense out of people. It would be a good idea, I told myself, to show this film to the mouthing dictators, the drifting politicians, the youngsters who sigh in secret for a new and exciting life, the old men who at heart are ready for a sensation even at the expense of millions of lives. When they all begin to talk about the stout-hearted legions of patriots, the honour of the nation, the necessity for expansion, and the rest of it, let them be shown this film at once, I thought, and told it is this they are wanting all over again. (Though if the worst and loudest of them were at once hustled into a shallow trench and then shelled and bombed by a battery and squadron appointed by the League of Nations, it might be still more effective.) Then I saw that this film would not serve such a purpose, or at least would not serve it as well as it might be served. No film, no matter how realistic in its conception and execution, can suggest the muddle and monotony, the waste without end, the long obscenities of war. *Verdun*, after all, is art, and it is too cleanly tragic. It has beauty, a dangerous beauty.

It is a film full of great things, but perhaps the greatest is the Fort Vaux episode. The ceaseless bombardment, the hand-to-hand fighting, the gas attacks, all were superbly pictured, and it was impossible to believe that these men of the beleagured garrison, which still held out when the Germans were actually holding the top of the fort, were merely playing parts. We sat there, choky and hot-eyed, watching them trying to signal, rationing out the last drops of water, and then saw, at last, the final surrender, when the French commandant surrendered his sword through the window and the Germans presented arms as the survivors of the heroic garrison reeled past. It was horrible, horrible; that fort was a hell; and yet I for one found in it all a queer fascination, like that of the ground that had been shelled over and over again, until it was as remote from humanity as the face of the moon, horrible, hellish, but with a terrible austere beauty of its own. It holds my imagination yet, thunders there like the last scene of *Hamlet*. The men who made this film were soldiers, and there runs through it that grave pride of soldiers. Verdun was one of those places—the very emperor of them—that made all its visitors Freemen; when you had been there you knew you had got down to bedrock and that after that you could shrug your shoulders at the worst hell the theologians ever invented: you had 'been through it.' Every man who did any real soldiering knows what I mean; he remembers that strange ecstasy. He also knows, as I know, that it will not do. That is why *Verdun* will not do simply as a piece of anti-war propaganda; it is too high and clean and tragic for that. But what a film! When I caught sight of M. Leon Poirier, its creator, afterwards, I had quite a shock. It was as if one had just run up against Prospero, a Prospero who had exchanged the enchanted island for a blasted heath.

O<small>N THE</small> last ninth of November nearly everybody here had a fantastic time of it. This is what happened to me in the morning, quite early too, before ten o'clock. I went to see a man in a white coat, and he made me lie back in a huge chair, and then another man in a white coat covered my nose and mouth with a horrible black bag. I found I could not breathe properly, had one second of appalling panic, but then seemed to recover, for I remember telling somebody that this black bag business was a great mistake. Who this somebody was I do not know, but it was not either of the men in white coats. I saw them after this other mysterious conversation had ended, and they were smiling and telling me it was all over and handing me tumblers of warm pinkish stuff. Five ivory bits of me were lying in a row on a table near by. I am not the same man that first sat in that chair—or if I am, then indeed we are immortal creatures. It is queer how inconsistent we are. When we are reading sad and learned little books, we are ready to agree with their

authors that we are nothing but a bright conference of particles, so much blood and bone and
hair on the move; but in our ordinary talk we
quietly assume that we are immortal beings, here
with a body for a season. We say, 'I have had
some teeth out,' just as if the teeth were not really
a part of us; and we shed an appendix or a gall-
bladder, a leg or an arm, but allow what remains
of us to go on saying 'I' all the time as if we were
just the same. This should be looked into, I feel.

When I returned home, I discovered that the
prospect of leaving the house again that day did
not appeal to me. Indeed, it was understood that
I should stay in, and I spent the rest of the morning and all the afternoon either mixing more of
the warm pinkish stuff or picking up books, staring at a page or two, then putting them down
again. It is a fine thing to have at your elbow a
pile of good new books, but somehow the least
suggestion of pain in the face seems to make it
impossible to read such new books. The publishers' superlatives are hardly dry on the paper
jackets: 'This brilliant . . .'; 'Undoubtedly the
greatest . . .'; 'The rarest of all . . .'; 'An un-
forgettable . . .'; and all true, entirely just, well-
deserved; but somehow I could not bother to read

them. I did not have a miserable day. One rarely does have a really miserable day. There is a certain pleasure in being a man who has just had five teeth out, a mixer of pinkish stuff. But I was not pleased when I learned at tea-time that I had 'missed it.' Missing it is hateful, and nothing makes me more angry than the thought that all manner of things may happen in the universe before long and I shall probably know nothing about them. At this moment there may be solar systems, dozens of planets whirling about green or purple suns, that have evolved a life even more fantastic and entertaining than ours, and yet you and I are in the dark about it all and will for ever stay in the dark. It is maddening.

Not that I believe for one second that I missed as much as they said I did. Their story was altogether too fantastic, and I suspect they concocted most of it on the way home. But this is what happened. On that Friday there was an expedition from this house to see the Lord Mayor's Show. The party included two little girls, Angela and Barbara, and a much larger girl, Suzette, who has just arrived from France; and it was they who told me all about it at tea-time. Now it is true that Suzette is tremendously old, grown-up—for she is eighteen—but nevertheless I believe she too was in the conspiracy. I admit that I did not hear much of the story from her, for when she speaks English she is so very slow that I forget the words at the beginning of the sentence long before she has reached the end, and when she speaks French she is so quick that it all runs together and I can only make out things like 'Tiens' and 'Alors,' things that do not mean very much. Over there in France, however, they have a passion for mayors and would do anything for a Lord Mayor, so that I can well believe that Suzette was in the conspiracy.

That they saw policemen and soldiers and boy scouts and heard a lot of bands playing, I have no difficulty in believing. I may not have ever seen the Lord Mayor's Show, but I have seen dozens and dozens of processions and they nearly always have soldiers and boy scouts and bands in them. Nothing was said about clean coal wagons, but if I know anything about processions, they were there too. I am ready to believe too that there was a huge milk bottle carried down the street, and a car filled with fruit, and another car showing a dirty house and a clean house. So far, so good. But now we come to some very dubious stuff. What about all those little toy soldiers? And King Alfred—what was he doing there? And that ship—how could there be a ship sailing down Fleet Street? And when we come to the Lord Mayor himself, it gets queerer and queerer. Nobody can make me believe that the Lord Mayor of London, a contemporary of yours and mine, a fellow citizen and ratepayer, an alderman, and—to crown all—a cricketer and the head of the Polytechnic in Regent Street, rode through the streets of this city in a gilded coach drawn by six horses, a coach like Cinderella's, only much larger. Of course, if you are going to admit the coach, there is no sense in trying to keep out the pleasant little additions to the legend, the accounts of coachmen and footmen in white wigs and gold lace, trumpeters in purple velvet. Once you have passed the golden fairy tale coach, you might as well let them all come, coachmen, footmen, trumpeters, bowmen, knights in armour, alchemists, and I know not what. Except the two giants, Gog and Magog, for even if I am driven to believe in the coach and the rest, I will not swallow the story of the giants.

There was some difference of opinion here about the giants. Barbara, the smallest member of the

party, said that they were real. In answer to a
query by a still younger sister (so small that she
stayed at home), Barbara gave it as her considered judgment that these were not the kind of
giants that make a practice of eating people, especially very little girls, who have to hide their
heads in the bed-clothes at night when the mischievous cry goes up in the nursery, 'Giants coming!' No, they were friendly fellows who had
merely asked to be allowed to join in the procession. But there was no doubt they were real because you saw their eyes move. Angela, however,
declared that they were not real giants but 'made-
up things with men in their legs'. I refuse to
believe they were either one or the other, that
any giants were there. If I allowed myself to
believe it, I should cry with vexation. The hours
and hours I have spent in that miserable Fleet
Street, never seeing anybody go up and down it
but advertising men, sub-editors, specialists in the
off-set process, reviewers, business managers of *The
Rabbit World* and *The Evangelist's Companion*,
all hurrying towards whisky-and-splashes or re-
luctantly leaving whisky-and-splashes, and all
looking alike; with nothing in the street itself
but a roaring pack of 11 and 13 buses and taxis

and vans full of soda-water or empty biscuit tins! And then these people sneak off one morning to this same Fleet Street and find it all festooned with flags and clashing with cymbals, with not an advertising man or bus in sight, and then see a procession of people from fairy tales and nursery rhymes parade its length, gold coaches, giants, and all! No, I will never believe that.

I must confess, though, that I was a little shaken when, in the evening, I read that the present Lord Mayor is an alderman of the Ward of Farringdon, or Farndone Without, the only ward that elects an alderman for the Within and an alderman for the Without. I could not help having an uneasy feeling that these stories I heard might be true after all, for when your alderman comes from a place called Farndone Without, obviously anything might happen. Then I remembered that former Lord Mayor, Dick Whittington, and it struck me then that the City of London is really a fairy tale and nursery rhyme sort of place. But I held on, accepting nothing stranger than a boy scout.

I DO not know exactly what I expected to find at Olympia, when I went there on the first afternoon of the Universal Cookery and Food Exhibition, but I do know that I did not find it. I arrived at West Kensington—that strangely remote and sinister district—when it was blowing a gale and the rain was lashing the streets and everybody was running hard, head downward. The lights of Olympia looked very cheerful, comforting, and I think it must have been when I was racing the last hundred yards that I entertained false visions of what would happen inside the place. Perhaps I had a fleeting picture of the vast hall of Olympia all succulent and steaming. The programme of the Exhibition encourages such visions, for on the front page is a spirited sketch of a chef holding up a pan and dipping a spoon into it. A beautiful smile lights up his face, and there is no doubt whatever that he is at your service, is preparing something, and that in another minute you will sit down and enjoy whatever there is in that pan. I think I imagined the whole Exhibition to be like that, seeing myself walking down long aisles, one for soup, one for fish, and so forth, all crowded with enthusiastic cooks begging me to try something. By the time I arrived at the turnstile, my mouth was watering.

Olympia, I am afraid, is too Olympian. It is so big that it immediately takes the character out of anything that happens there. I must have been, in my time, to four or five exhibitions there, all different, but they all looked alike, squatting beneath that colossal glass roof. Why I should have imagined that the cooks would break this spell, I do not know, but they certainly didn't. Their exhibition looked exactly like all the other exhibitions, at least in the general effect. No savoury steam rose to the dim glass above. No genial mob of white-capped chefs, begging me to sample their latest masterpieces, was anywhere to be seen. I do not say it would have been impossible to have something for nothing there. I was invited to sample some Virol-and-milk, some custard, some ginger wine, and brown bread, all of which I politely and mournfully refused. A man does not creep into the shadow of M. Escoffier to taste such things. At first, indeed, I could not see any food. The stalls seemed to be all given up to machinery and uniforms and printing and shop equipment and other dismal matters. A large determined man insisted upon demonstrating to me a new and ingenious trouser-press and finally compelled me to buy one, though I did not want a trouser-press. A severe young woman handed me a pamphlet and before I had time either to look at it or to go away she began a passionate monologue on the subject of arrowroot, about which I have always been—mistakenly perhaps—completely indifferent. I lingered for a moment at a stall where carrots and other vegetables had been cut into fantastic shapes, but a man hurried forward with a glitter in his eye and a patent kitchen knife (10 different uses) in his hand, and I slunk away.

Then I discovered a young man who was actually engaged in cooking something; at least I saw him put some vegetables and a piece of meat into a kind of stew-pot. This was no ordinary stew-pot, however, for it apparently had something to do with high steam pressure. 'No water needed,' I heard the young man say. 'The vegetables are cooked in their own steam.' I drifted away, for I am not a man who can find any interest in Brussels sprouts, even though every sprout is artfully led on to cook himself in his own steam, at four in the afternoon. And I did not even linger at the stall where a facetious young lady, with a manner faintly reminiscent of Marie Lloyd, demonstrated how things could be fried in some new sort of oil. She gave me the impression that she had been standing before audiences, frying-pan in hand, day in and day out for the last six months. If at once you don't succeed, fry, fry again, she must have been telling herself. Not very far away was a table piled with pamphlets all about the Army; there was a full-blown recruiting sergeant in attendance; and to the right of the table, not two yards from the sergeant, was a mysterious dark doorway. I disliked the look of these arrangements; they wore a sinister air; and I asked myself why the Army should come recruiting in such an exhibition, why the sergeant had found this rather dark corner; and I decided that there was probably a plot to spirit away young chefs, who would remember being asked to peep inside the dark doorway and then would remember nothing until they found themselves in a mess kitchen in Aldershot.

It was not until I reached the very centre of the vast hall that I understood what this Exhibition can really do. There, in all its glory, was the *Table d'Honneur,* where *les maîtres* exhibited their culinary trifles. They were magnificent but they were not the food. It was impossible to imagine yourself eating one of these astonishing exhibits. I never quite understood what most of them were made of or how they could possibly have been concocted. That Chinese garden—for example—a trifling dish two yards long by one broad—containing a pagoda, bridge and stream, summerhouse, trees in bloom, flower-beds and paths, mandarins and ducks, all as gaily coloured as an Oriental print—you could stare at it and admire it, but how could you possibly eat it? Suppose you were the host and this astounding dish was brought in by four staggering waiters—what could you do about it? Would you attack it with knife, fork, or spoon? And where would you begin? To give one person quarter of the pagoda roof, a branch of the cherry tree, a couple of ducks, to give another half a bridge, a bit of flower-bed, and some garden path, this would be unthinkable. I will never believe such things were ever meant to be eaten. Lucullus himself would never have dared to plunge a tablespoon into them.

There were innumerable dishes of this sort, people, buildings, birds and animals, whole scenes, all cunningly shaped and coloured. I think my favourites were some trays packed tight with tiny baskets filled with every imaginable kind of *hors d'œuvres*. Even these, however, had a glazed and varnished look, and, like the rest, suggested wooden toys rather than food. It would have been great fun to have seen some very bold and irreverent person suddenly produce a knife and fork and eat one of these exhibits, but I could not imagine a knife or fork penetrating them. What I could imagine was the horror of the assembled *maîtres*, for it was here that you found the chefs, serious but loquacious Latins, with bowler hats, tiny beards, and ribbons in their button-holes. This was the opening day of their Academy. Were they deciding what was to be the dish of the year? I don't know, but I am still ready to give my vote for the Chinese garden.

After that somehow I contrived to see quite a lot of food, mostly light and sweet stuff. There were rows of exquisite *gateaux*, delicious riots of chocolate and almond icing, whole orchards of marzipan fruit, trays of *petit fours glaces* and bonbons, macaroons and raspberry sponges, and the most tempting rolls of Vienna bread. And what happened after I had stared at all these delicacies?

I will tell you. I visited a dingy marble counter, brother to all those that you and I have visited in railway-station refreshment rooms, and demanded a cup of tea. This cup of tea came from an urn and tasted, as usual, of liquorice and warm leather. 'Will you have a bun with it?' the girl at the counter asked, and she indicated a glass case full of those buns that are only to be found in railway refreshment rooms. 'I will *not* have a bun, thank you,' I replied politely and sadly; and, taking my cup of tea in my hand, I turned my back on the counter and surveyed, without enthusiasm, what I could see from there of the Thirty-First Universal Cookery and Food Exhibition. 'By this time,' I told myself, 'they are probably awarding the gold and silver medals for Raised Game and other pies, for Petit Fours, Gateaux and Patisseries, for Nouille Paste and Fancy Meringue Work. I'm going home.' A useful, interesting, *good* exhibition, undoubtedly, but rather—a little—I don't quite know what to say—stand-offish, perhaps.

SUPER-SUPER

THE super-super kinema has arrived. I have been inside it. They call it The Empire and it stands exactly where our old acquaintance stood, on the north side of Leicester Square. But let nobody imagine it is the same place. These two Empires have their roots in two different continents, for the old music-hall was essentially European and the new kinema is undoubtedly American. No, they do not belong to the same age, perhaps not to the same civilization. A social historian might do worse than begin a gigantic study of our times with an artful reference to the fall of the old Empire and the sudden rise of the new.

I had never seen this new place until the other afternoon, when its blaze of light drew me through the drizzle and murk of Leicester Square. I paid one-and-sixpence (the lowest price) and found myself in a colossal and sumptuous entrance hall. There was a vast central candelabra, studded with bright globes of russet gold, and a host of similar globes illuminated the rich walls. Everywhere the decorations seemed to be in chocolate and gold,

« 189 »

a symbolic combination. You saw immense marble balustrades curving up into some mysterious and still more opulent region beyond. Your feet were nearly lost in the carpets. There seemed to be a small chocolate army of attendants. Turning to the left, still on the ground floor, I found myself in a great lounge and tea-room, about as big as the railway station in a provincial town. There were five people eating and drinking there—or it might have been fifty—or five hundred—I did not stop to count them and any number might have seemed a handful in that room. I left a bag in the cloak-room, after being assured by at least three attendants, who had nothing much to do and were getting anxious, that there was no charge, no charge whatever. I had a wash, a free wash, in a massive and spotless lavatory that offered me hot water, soap, and a pile of clean towels. They looked such good towels that I had a shock when I discovered they were made of paper, and I had to use four of them before I was completely dry. Perhaps if I had asked for something to eat and drink, I should have been given that for nothing too, and if I had, I should not have been surprised. As I returned to the main hall, left the golden globes behind, and climbed stairs sumptuous in chocolate and gilt, I began to feel that I had wandered into the Arabian Nights.

When I reached the kinema itself, I was certain that my eighteen-pence had conjured me into something like the Baghdad of Haroun al-Raschid. My ticket admitted me into the Circle. And what a Circle! It made me dizzy. I could not see the beginning of it. A mediæval artist would have thought it had been contrived for the Last Judgement. You could comfortably put the population of half a dozen villages into it. When I entered the whole place was shaking with sickly-sweet sound that seemed to come now from one side, now from another. Far below was a kind of gilded box illuminated by several searchlights, and then I noticed that a man was doing something to this box. He was playing it. It was an organ, an organ mysteriously suspended in mid-air. If I had been stone-deaf, I should have delighted in that fantastic instrument, but unfortunately I could hear only too well and I hated the sound of it.

When the organ faded from bright to dim gold and finally sank out of sight as well as out of hearing, there was a blessed interval of silence. It was followed by the sound of an orchestra, a large and enthusiastic orchestra. I craned my neck, but could see no orchestra. The next minute, however, I caught sight of the necks of three double-basses. Then the whole orchestra came into view; more and more lights came on magically; the trombones blared and the cymbals clashed; and this crazy orchestra still rose and rose. Old John Sebastian Bach himself would have muttered a short prayer at the sight of such a marvel, though when they had finished their two cheap and noisy items, he might have had a word or two to say to some of the instrumentalists. Still, there it was —a good large orchestra, big enough to tackle a symphony. After that, it accompanied the pictures, or rather, so far as I was concerned, it killed them. That is the trouble about music, it is so terribly real and urgent. You cannot make it the servant of a few flickering shadows on a screen. It blows their puling stuff to smithereens. You cannot show photographs of a pretty, vapid girl, pathetically imagining she is acting when she makes a few grimaces, and have fifty stout instrumentalists hard at work just below, sending out great gusts of joy and agony, and then expect those of us who have ears to bother our heads about the picture.

There was one space during which neither organ nor orchestra was visible and audible. If this had been truly the Arabian Night it resembled, I should say that during that time we were entertained by a demon or ifrit. And really that is the best way of describing the monstrous thing that happened. We were shown on the screen some curtains and from somewhere behind there came the most dreadful sounds, as if our orchestra, now out of sight, had gone to hell and could be heard lamenting there. After a minute or two of this, the photographed curtains parted to show us a stage, and on to the stage came a black man about eighteen feet high. He pranced about, took off his hat, put it on again, got down on his knees, and all the time opened and shut his cavernous mouth as if he were singing. And now into those strange sounds from behind there came a kind of voice, howling and moaning something about 'a mel-o-dee from out of the South.' It was horrible, frightening.

What was most curious of all, however, was the fact that this great building, with its marble and carpets and candelabra and chocolate and gold, its changing coloured lights, its fantastic rising and falling orchestras, all its opulence and effort and superb ingenuity, was there to show those little bits of flickering nonsense on the screen.

It was as if a government should call out an army
corps to hunt down a few stray cats and dogs.
The films I saw were just the same kind of films
I have seen in adapted drill-halls and institutes
that had nothing but fifteen rows of seats, a screen,
a projector, and a tinny old piano. In such sur-
roundings, they did well enough, being a fair substitute for lantern lectures, amateur nigger minstrel
shows, or cantatas by the local chapel choir. One
went, was mildly amused for an hour or so, and
went yawning home. But that everything in this
immense, luxurious, and complicated palace should
be at the service of such poor things seemed to me
monstrous. To sit in that colossal circle, to hear
the thunder of the orchestra, to see the purple,
lilac, and orange lights change and fade, to watch
the velvet curtains on the stage sweep up, and then
—at the end of it all—to have nothing but a bit
of black-and-white moving photography—it was
preposterous. Any films, however good they were,
would have seemed absurd set in such a framework.
But the ones I saw were not good, they were of an
incredible stupidity. It is not that they were not
beautiful, tragic, richly comic, deeply significant;
they were not amusing; they were nothing, just
poor feeble vulgar little shadows. I left in the

middle of the most important one—the pretty, vapid girl was still grimacing and the orchestra was thundering away as if Hamlet was lying dead in Elsinore—and as I climbed the steep cliff of the Circle, descended the chocolate and gold stairs, walked under the great candelabra, I still felt rather dazed, like a man who had visited the British Museum and found there nothing but two or three egg-shells and a broken umbrella. I am still wondering, but I am not grumbling. There is nothing to grumble at in being given a slice of the Arabian Nights for one-and-sixpence.

A NEW TOBACCO

THE best thing that has happened here these last few days has been the arrival, through the post, of two pound tins of tobacco. Not that these were a gift; no such luck comes my way. I often receive copies of new books from publishers, yet nobody ever sends me a review tin of new tobacco. Why is that? I am far more interested in new brands of smoking mixtures than I am in new samples of poetry or fiction mixtures. Why is it that people are so lavish with books, of which there are far, far too many in the world, and so mean about other things? Why cannot we have a weekly paper that reviews everything and not merely books? After all, who really *cares* about books? Let us have a paper that notices all the new things—wine, tobacco, hats, chairs, typewriters, gramophones, pianolas, and so on and so forth. Some of the things, of course, would not be really new; the wine, for example, would be old, but fresh samples would be sent in from time to time in order that the fortunate reviewer (for we will still call him that and not 'taster') might call attention once more to its virtues. On such a paper I would readily engage to do the pipe-tobacco column, and do it too in the good old style: 'Among the younger Virginias, Smith's Light is rapidly,' etc.; 'Brown's is quickly proving itself a mixture to be reckoned with'; 'Once you have taken up Dreadnought Plug, you cannot put it down—or keep it down.' What a change it would be to have my table filled with strange bright tins of tobacco instead of books in gaudy jackets bristling with publishers' lies!

Now the tobacconists from whom I ordered these two pound tins steer clear of the bounce and brag and downright lying that is all too common in the literary, theatrical, musical and other worlds of to-day. They write me a modest little letter, in which they remark, 'It is not for us to sing the praises of this tobacco, but we think you will find that it has an unusually fine flavour, and it is absolutely pure'; which is, after all, more than you could say of some of our recent attempts at literature, which are described as if they were the very summit of man's achievement on this planet. But what was I doing to be ordering tobacco in this way? The fact is, I made a most romantic discovery. For some time now, believing that a man should have some object in life, I have been looking for a pure Virginia, a quest that sounds, I think, sufficiently romantic in itself. Like many of my idle day-dreaming egotistical tribe, I am a heavy pipe-smoker, having long found it necessary to stupefy myself with tobacco in order not to feel too acutely the pangs of injured vanity, the shame of poverty and obscurity, and the constant prickings of a Nonconformist conscience. However, I will not apologize for my pipe, for man, being terribly burdened with a consciousness, must dope himself in one way or another, and if he is not smoking or drinking he is making illicit love or denouncing something or somebody, delivering a message to all thinking men, passing unnecessary laws, drugging himself with a sense of power; so that it seems to me that my way of escaping the tedium of being conscious or the pain of thought is perhaps the least guilty, for smoky and blackened though I may be, I am at least amiable, puffing away.

Now my taste in tobacco inclines towards the Oriental. I delight in your full mixtures that are dark and heavily fragrant with Latakia and Perique, mixtures that hold the gorgeous East in fee.

A NEW TOBACCO

There was a time—you may say it was during my decadent period—when, determined to live only for the splendid moment, I smoked Latakia alone, like one of Ouida's heroes. Nor can I actually say that it seemed to do me any harm—though even tobacconists, who must make a handsome profit out of the stuff, cautioned me against it and regarded me as a chef might who was told that I ate nothing but Christmas pudding—but it is supposed to be bad for the heart and it is certainly rather cloying. Since then, I have tried innumerable tobaccos, but have usually kept to the full-flavoured mixtures that have one foot at least in Asia. Nevertheless I have always felt (prompted perhaps by some Puritan ancestor) that a man who smoked as much as I do should content himself with a pure Virginia. You notice that I do not give the adjective an initial capital: every sensible pipe-smoker will know why: pure Virginia tells you exactly what I wanted to find the shape of the thing in my thoughts, and 'Pure Virginia' does not. For some time, then, this has been my quest, undertaken without any flourish of trumpets, pursued quietly yet indefatigably. Unlike so many contemporaries of mine in authorship, bright but disillusioned fellows, I have had an object in life, and I do not hesitate to say that it has sustained me through many periods of great trial. It has also taken me into a great many queer little tobacconists' shops and filled my pouch and pipe with some very foul-smelling and evil-tasting stuff. It ever a man deserved the freedom of the city from Richmond, Va., merely for smoking his pipe, then I am that man. But there is, of course, plenty of respectable Virginia tobacco in the world, and I tried a number of brands that were fit to be smoked but that always stopped short of perfection, being too mild and monotonous, too heavy and parching, or, like the Clown's ginger, hot i' the mouth. Once or twice, even after a week's industrious smoking, I imagined that I had found what I wanted at last, that I need go no further, yet always my fancy went straying on, discovering that here was not perfection; and I would go back to my mixtures, never keeping to the same one long, or I would make further experiments with Virginia.

Such was the position when we motored back from the north the other week. I was still hopeful

but a little subdued, beginning to trifle with disillusion or to turn Platonic and console myself
with the thought of ideal Plugs and Navy Cuts.
Now comes the stroke of fate or chance that is
to be found in all good romantic narratives. We
broke our journey down the Great North Road
at Doncaster, and there I discovered that I had
no tobacco at all. I did not regard this as a real
opportunity for research but simply as the domestic crisis so familiar to all smokers, and I
hurried across to the nearest tobacconist's as any
common puffer of pipes, your nearest ounce-
packet man, might have done. The shop was
rather small and in no way to be distinguished
from the ordinary. It happened, however, that the
assistant was engaged when I entered and that
gave me an opportunity, all too rare in these
shops, to look round, or 'browse', as they say in
the bookshops. There was time for the mere hasty
desire for fuel to be shredded away and clarified,
for the instincts of the connoisseur, the collector,
the explorer, to assert themselves. I cast about
for a Virginia that held out the slightest promise,
and when the assistant, who was a middle-aged
man and not the all too frequent contemptuous

female, came to attend to me, I asked him a few questions. The result was that I departed, sceptically, I must confess, carrying a quarter-pound tin of tobacco that he strongly recommended, a fine-cut rather dark Virginia. This tobacco is all that he said it was, very cool, sweet but not cloying (and therefore unlike those American plugs that seem to glisten with sugar and are like toffee), fairly lasting in spite of its being fine-cut; so good indeed that, as you know, I have just ordered two pounds of it and am puffing away at them this very moment.

I believe that I have found the tobacco I have long been looking for, but that does not mean that I shall necessarily stick to it. I have been told over and over again that it is better to keep to one brand of tobacco, and I am always meeting men who have 'never smoked anything else for thirty years, y'know' and never fail to admire their constancy, while admitting that I am the very Casanova of pipe-smokers. There is, however, something to be said for this chopping and changing. If you are for ever smoking something new, trying another brand or returning to it to see how it stands in comparison with the last you

«202»

had, you contrive to raise what is generally a mere habit into a conscious pleasure. Most smokers—and this is certainly true of cigarette smokers—have what might be called a negative attitude and not a positive one towards the practice, by which I mean that they smoke only in order to free themselves from the restlessness and dissatisfaction they feel when not smoking. Now I do not say that I, who am equally a creature of the habit, would not feel such restlessness and dissatisfaction if I were deprived of my tobacco, but I do say that when I am smoking I am not merely, as it were, brought up to zero from a point below it. I am tasting and enjoying the tobacco all the time, fully conscious of its defects and excellences; and this is because I am for ever making experiments. And is it not strange that so little has been written about tobacco and the adventures of the smoker? I never come across anything on the subject except those general eulogies of the weed quoted so often by tobacconists, and purely technical treatises that mean nothing to people outside the trade. It is just as if all statements about books could be divided into observations such as that by Carlyle comparing a library to a university, and remarks about printing, proofreading and binding. Why does not some enthusiastic but critical smoker artfully describe his traffic with the pipe, his nights of Latakia, Perique, Virginia? When so much is ending in it, why cannot we have a volume or two on smoke?

A VANISHED LODGING

MY COLLEGE at Cambridge, attempting improvements in the far court, has pulled down the tiny lodge at the back gate. Now I 'kept' in this lodge for a brief season. And there goes another link with the past, and with it, I fear, my chance of fame in Cambridge. While that lodge existed, was pointed at, I was somebody, for I was the man who once 'kept' in it. To call my three years at Cambridge a career is to flatter them. Never were nine terms passed with less distinction. My academic honours were trumpery, and though I once gained an essay prize, to the splendid tune of fifteen pounds, I think it was because I was the only competitor. I was never chosen for any team or crew, and therefore never received any colours or ties or painted oars. My voice was never heard at the Union, and no honourable proposer was ever butchered by wit of mine. I never even edited an undergraduate paper. The demigods who came from town to look us over showed no desire to take me up or even to make my acquaintance. My name was never whispered over common-room port as that of a coming man. Being then, as now, neither handsome, nor rich nor charming nor even particularly amiable, I was never in demand anywhere and could show a mantelpiece touchingly bare of invitation cards. I crept through those three years like a mouse, that is, if you can imagine a pipe-smoking, beer-drinking, dogmatic and intolerant mouse. Nevertheless, I could boast of one distinction, or at least one singularity. For two terms I had the queerest rooms in all the University. I may have been a nonentity, but nobody can deny me my queerest rooms. I was lodged like an elf.

Now that the little place has been pulled down, I shall not be believed. I cannot take my children there and climb with them up the curling iron staircase, so droll and Lilliputian that they would have adored it. I can only play with my memories of it. Let me begin at the beginning. My college, one of the smaller ones, was full and my name had found its way into the book only at the last moment. It was a rule there that you spent the first year in college, so some place had to be found for me although all the rooms were taken. But my very first term was not spent in the back gate lodge. No, I went first to what was called the

Tutor's House, a house intended for a married don but at that time occupied by two single ones. Here a bedroom and a sitting-room were found for me. I can remember that sitting-room now, very large and very bare (for I had only about three sticks of furniture) and perishingly cold; the Spartan little lunches of bread and cheese; and myself there, sitting in overcoat, sometimes reading about the Holy Roman Empire, and sometimes staring at the dead leaves in the garden, like a man in a Russian short story. Something may have told the college authorities—perhaps my forlorn and overcoated figure appeared to them night after night in clear dreams—that all was not well with me; or again (and this is more likely) they may have decided that those rooms would serve other and nobler purposes; but I was informed that the following term would see me elsewhere. When I returned, I was shown the back gate lodge. The back gate, you see, was never opened, so that its toy lodge had been empty and idle for years. I can only describe it by saying that it was like the smallest cottage that you ever saw, only that it had fantastic iron corkscrew stairs outside. Up those stairs was my front door, and behind that door were two miniature rooms.

It was indeed an elfin habitation, and I think I was very happy there. Sixteen weeks were just long enough; after that it would have been all inconvenience and swearing; but as it was I did not outstay the wonder of it. A man could not live a couple of terms in such a place and be dull. It heightened mere living, eating and drinking and going to bed, into the high fantastical. Indeed, I never quite convinced myself that everything was real, and to the very last, when I walked down those shaky and curling stairs for ever, I half felt as if I were living in a dream. The isolation of the little place was both queer and attractive. You were in college and yet not in college. Then there was the approach, those absurd stairs. However dull and commonplace you might feel walking across the court, all that disappeared when you began to mount your stairs, for you climbed into mingled absurdity and romance and so came home kindling. Then there were the rooms themselves. The bedroom I remember as a pretty little trifle, with honeysuckle outside the leaded window, but as I only went there to sleep—at the last possible moment—it plays no great part in my remembrance. It is the sitting-room that catches my eye. My visitors—and I could only have one at a time—must have thought they were creeping into a tobacco tin. It was diminutive to the pitch of fantasy, a place for a friendly pair of leprechauns. Electricity had not reached this place of mine, though the rest of the college had it, but there was gas, and I remember a gas mantle rather smaller than my thumb and not more than five feet from the floor. The gas-fire I had installed would not have seemed amiss in the Queen's Dolls' House. A table there was and so small that I had only to put two coffee cups and a tin of biscuits on it to fill it and give the impression I was providing a feast.

It happened, too, that at that time I was buying a great many books, the fruits of a weekly prowl round all the bookshops and the stalls in the market square. You can see me, very knowing, in front of the shilling and sixpenny boxes. Sometimes I plunged a little—I did for a set of Elizabethan dramatists, not one of whom I ever want to read now—but as a rule I disregarded everything marked above five shillings, and my average purchase was about eighteen-pence, so that I soon came to have a very ragged regiment of friends. Some of my greatest bargains I have regretted since. One was a set of the *Waverley Novels,* large and heavy volumes, bound in the remains of calf and with any number of plates, all showing dark and somehow quite incredible places, the very set that every gentleman of the 'Forties would select for his library. Undoubtedly I paid very little for these massive volumes, but I have paid enough in carriage and cartage since for them to buy several sets, of a size suitable for a reader and not a weight-lifter. I remember that these *Waverly Novels*, along with a host of other dogs'-eared and battered books, found their way up to my little room. Shelves were not to be thought of, and so the books had to be piled up all round the walls, and as more and more arrived, the piles grew higher and higher and thicker and thicker, reaching under the table, until at last I could never find a volume I wanted nor hardly force an entrance into the room at all. Even before, if another pipe-smoker spent the evening with me— taking turns in the solitary armchair—we lost one another completely in the thick blue smoke after half an hour or so. But I had my visitors, and how I talked there!—or rather, indulged in that mixture of brag, day-dreaming, and ignorant dogmatism which passes among young males for talk.

During my first term there, which was the

Easter one, I was very snug indeed, for the worst enemy of these rooms (and obviously they never had one) could not deny they were cosy. In the summer term, which was unusually warm, this cosiness unfortunately persisted. I only remember one hotter room than mine in Cambridge that term, and that was the Examination Hall in which we were cabined stiflingly for a week when the sun was at its very height. It is monstrous that young men (I say nothing about young women; they seem to take kindly to examinations) should be asked to spend a week of their time answering these stupid questions:

> O, Cuckoo! shall I call thee bird,
>   Or but a wandering voice?
> State the alternative preferred,
>   Give reasons for your choice.

It is more monstrous still that blue midsummer should be chosen as the time of ordeal. I delight in hot weather and ask for nothing better than to bask in the sunshine; but I must not be expected to think, must not be questioned about the Holy Roman Empire or the Idealistic Theory of the State. I cannot be hot and intelligently communicative at one and the same time. Thus it was that the heat that term put me out of all

« 211 »

sympathy with examiners, and by the third day I was replying with savage irony to their idiotic queries, and by the fifth day I was replying not at all. But I could not keep cool in my absurd little room, though I sat there, clad only in pyjamas, drinking beer chill from the buttery. I sat up, night after night, sweating away, as if I were an engineer on a tramp in the Indian Ocean. Indeed, it was not unlike being on a ship. The little curly iron staircase, which was quite hot itself during the last few weeks, might have come straight out of a ship's engine-room. Thus it will be seen how my lodging offered opportunities to the fancy, unlike the common set of rooms, mere boxes for eating and sleeping. I enjoyed myself there, and I think the other men in the college rather enjoyed my being there; the sight of me, climbing or descending those stairs, always amused them; and men from other colleges came specially to have a look at the place. Now they have pulled down my elfin home, and with the last brick has vanished my one claim to academic distinction. I'll to the Cam no more, the laurels all are cut.

MODES

THE work that inspired the above title is called *Modes and Manners of the Nineteenth Century*. It is in four volumes and published by Messrs. Dent. I recommend these four volumes, which have themselves a sort of boudoir look, to the remaining few who have still time to browse with books, idly to turn over pages and stare at pictures. That is what I have been doing for several hours to-day. I have been looking at the pictures in these volumes, and there are hundreds and hundreds of them. They kill the letterpress, which, so far as I can judge by dipping into it here and there, is quiet, earnest, intelligent, and painful, like the talk of cultured Germans. (It is, indeed, a German performance.) I open Volume II and my eye falls on this sentence: 'We know now that a constitution drawn up on the most liberal lines can do nothing in the hands of administrators who, supported by a reactionary bureaucracy, sycophantic judges, and a servile police, proved the head of the State with every means of carrying out his autocratic principles.'

And then I cannot read any more because just above and also on the page opposite there are pictures from *The Repository* of 1819, and one of them shows a girl playing a strange kind of harp and the other shows another girl in walking dress, with a green hat trimmed with ostrich feathers and a frilly white skirt that reaches from her ankles nearly to her neck. This girl has white stockings and little green shoes and is altogether charming. Nobody could read about 'a reactionary bureaucracy' in her presence; and I do not try, knowing very well that her little green shoes are worth a cartload of this third-rate political philosophizing.

Now I open Volume IV, quite—as the reviewers say, after they have spent an hour looking for a harmful quotation—at random. I read: 'On the Continent a period of nationalism followed the downfall of Napoleon. Each race sought political hegemony. The German, Italian, Greek, Bulgar, Serb, Rumanian attained it; the Czech, Pole, South Slav continually strove for it.' Then at once the pictures catch my eye and I know that I do not care a rap whether the Czech attained political hegemony or not. On that very page is a neat drawing labelled 'Bar In London, 1866,' and a fine bar it is too, with an officer, waisted and Ouida-ish, two gents with top hats and large moustaches and monocles and pipes, and an array of barmaids, all with curly fringes and busts magnificent in black silk. At the back there are any number of champagne bottles waiting to be opened. The place must be 'up West,' as they always said in the rowdy-dowdy songs, and I have no doubt it was invaluable to young men bent on 'seeing life'—for they were great on seeing life in those days. On the opposite page, in the full glory of plate paper and colour, is a portrait of Mme. Jourdain, also 1886. She wears an evening gown that looks like a tulip, and long crimson gloves, and is even more adorable than the girl with the little green shoes. I hope her husband was not a descendant of the great M. Jourdain, for if he was he may not have realized that he was listening to Poetry (in long crimson gloves) every day of his life. And now you can understand why I do not trouble my head about the letterpress. It is written in such a style that it was half-dead when it was born, and the pictures simply finish it off. Let us turn to the pictures.

There are, as I remarked before, hundreds and hundreds of them, and they are nearly all pictures

of women, from fashion plates, portraits, draw-
ings of the *Punch* variety, photographs, anything,
in short, that will show us a woman in the fash-
ionable dress of a certain period. We move from
1790 to 1914. Here are our mothers and grandmothers and great-grandmothers and great-great-
grandmothers, all in their best clothes. Not that
men are excluded from this gallery of fashion.
We are there, too, but our clothes have changed
so little during this period that the editors very
rightly concluded that our sex was not worth more
than about one picture to every hundred or so of
the other sex. We have our cravats and whiskers
and tight trousers and loose trousers, but really
these things do not make much difference to us.
We are obviously the same people, brothers under
the skin; if you put us all in one room we should
get on very well together, cravats or no cravats,
whiskers or no whiskers. The editors were quite
right not to bother their heads about us. The
women repay them amply for their attention.

What a protean sex it is! I find it impossible
to believe that these hundreds of women are really
all more or less the same shape, that their actual
measurements probably do not vary beyond a few
inches this way or that. About every fifteen years

they seem to have changed into entirely different
beings: they might have been imported from various other planets. Sometimes they are very tall
and willowy, sometimes they are short, broad and
plump. Now they all look straight-haired, demure
or grave, and intent upon good works; now they
suddenly blossom out into curls and frills and
naughtiness. You cannot imagine the women of
one fashion being able to communicate with those
of any other. It is unbelievable that one of these
Empire style women, so tall and straight, high-
waisted and long-legged, could be the mother of
one of these pyramid-shaped creatures of the
'fifties, with her tiny bonnet and vast sweep of
crinoline. If we could put this girl of 1834, who
has a poke bonnet and little curls, bare shoulders,
enormous sleeves that seem to begin where most
sleeves end, and the waist of a wasp, into the
same room with this girl of 1912, who begins
with a colossal hat and then narrows down to a
few inches at her ankles, we do not believe that
they could possibly have a word to say to one
another. They all seem to live in different worlds.
Nothing, indeed, so swiftly evokes the spirit of
an age than a picture or two of its fashionably
dressed women. Instantly, you see the whole back-

ground and entertain a hurried, confused but rich vision of the period, its social life, literature, art, music, ideals and idiocies. And it is easy to see why these mere fashion plates should be so evocative: nothing could be more in and of its age than women's dress; it is here, everywhere, to-day and gone for ever to-morrow; so that whole chapters on the Crimean and the Mutiny, Palmerston and Cobden, Tennyson and Dickens and Thackeray, Millet and Frith, seem to tell us no more about the 'fifties than the sight of a single crinoline. That is why I like staring at these pictures, for they bring history to life with a ribbon or a flounce.

It is amusing to notice how one regards these fashions. Backward from 1914 to about 1890, they seem odd and rather repulsive, being the cast-offs of yesterday, the stuff of lumber-rooms and mildewing old trunks. After that they begin to be touched by romance, just as the knee-length dresses, the tiny hats, the flesh-coloured silk stockings, of our own day will seem movingly pictur-esque, romantic, to the people, dressed Heaven knows how, of 1987. I will put a bold face upon it and say outright that I do not like the fashions of to-day. They may be more convenient—all

women say they are, though I do not believe
women really care twopence for convenience—but
they seem to me rather monotonous in their
straightness and legginess, and—what is more important—only suitable for á relatively small por-
tion of the sex. The young girl of to-day can
crow over her older sisters and her mother and
her aunts because fashion has decreed that all
women shall wear dresses really intended for nobody but young slim boyish creatures, that Hera
and Aphrodite shall go disguised as Artemis. I am
not sure that women are not changing their characters simply to fit the clothes into which they
struggle. There is probably more in this than
in all the solemn nonsense about the 'new femi-
nism' and the 'new consciousness of sex.' Short
views came in with short skirts. Not that I have
any intention of falling into the old trap and
saying that girls are not what they were and asking where the purity and dignity and deep ma-
ternal affections of the women of yesterday are
to be found. I turn to the pictures here of the
women of the early 'sixties, and remark their
demure little bonnets and vast spread of skirts:
all of them look as if they had just been visiting
the sick and the poor and were about to feed a

favourite bird or read to their grandmothers. Now listen to this:

I do not mean to say that there are not now, as there always have been in every state of society, beautiful and amiable women, combining good sense and high principle; but there are too many who seem to have taken for their ideal a something between the dashing London horse-breaker and some Parisian *artiste dramatique*; the object of whose ambition is to be mistaken for a *femme du demi-monde*, to be insulted when they walk out with their petticoats girt up to their knees, shewing (to do them justice) remarkably pretty feet and legs, and to wearing wideawake hats over painted cheeks and brows, and walk with that indescribable, jaunty, 'devil-may-care' look which is considered 'the right thing' now-a-days—to make sporting bets—to address men as Jack, Tom, or Harry—to ride ahead in the Park— to call the paterfamilias 'governor,' and the lady mother 'the old party'—to talk of the young men who 'spoon' them, and discuss with them the merits of 'Skittles' and her horses, or the last scandalous story fabricated in the bay window at White's, the very faintest allusion to which would have made their mother's hair stand on end with dismay and horror:—this is to be pleasant, and 'fast' and amusing. . . . The girl of the year 1862 who is not 'fast' is generally dull and *blasée,* pleased with nothing, and possesses neither the wisdom of age nor the *naïveté* of youth.

So much for 1862. And the writer, no other than that old Regency Buck, Captain Gronow, heads the paragraph *Then and Now.* It is a good title and, as we know, may be used over and over again.

IT IS not true to say—as critics frequently do say—that flamboyant romantic literature is not like life. Where that literature departs from life is in being exciting, highly coloured, fantastic, all the time, in having no large blank spaces. But there are times when life can only be expressed in a flamboyant romantic fashion, for the fantastic stuff is there, under your nose. We may spend months in a world as quiet and prosaic as Jane Austen's and then suddenly we turn a corner— to find we have walked into the Dickens world. It happened to me only yesterday.

We are staying in a little town on the Kentish coast, an old-fashioned place but not Dickensy, far more reminiscent of *Black-Eyed Susan* and *All in the Downs* and songs by Dibdin. Yesterday morning we noticed an auctioneer's bill saying that the antique furniture and household effects of Lilac Cottage, all to be sold by auction, were on view that morning. We thought there would be no harm in looking over Lilac Cottage, which might have a wonderful little walnut bureau

or something of that sort tucked away in a corner
—you never know, do you? Nothing, you will
agree, could be more prosaic. We inquired our way
to Lilac Cottage, at the back of So-and-So Avenue.
It took a great deal of finding. We were passed
from one helpful but puzzled townsman to another; we tried third turnings to the right and
fourth turnings to the left for at least half an
hour. Finally, we came near, but even then spent
another ten minutes circling round the house. Our
last direction seemed to bring us to the railway
lines, but we discovered a very narrow little lane
running by the side of the railway, and at the
end of this lane a small gateway leading to a
garden that was a jungle of weeds. We crept
through gigantic briars and finally came to a little
old house. This was Lilac Cottage.

The threshold was simply so much rotten
wood; you could have crumbled it in your hand.
The interior was astonishing. I have never seen
so much dirt in all my life. Dust lay thick everywhere; huge cobwebs hung from the walls; and
every article of furniture was grimy beyond belief.
The atmosphere was choking. Long before you
dared to touch anything, your hand felt filthy.
All the women were stepping delicately from room

to room, holding their skirts. All the men smoked
furiously. You did not feel that the house had
just been opened but that it had just been ex-
humed. The two rooms on the ground floor and
the other two on the first floor were bad, but the
other little places, where nothing was being sold,
were horrors. I peeped into a kitchen in the base-
ment, and then fled. The very rats must have left
it years ago. And above there was a tiny bedroom—it had a bed in it and a straw mattress
completely covered with thick black dust—that
was a nightmare. In another little room I found
a man with a long moustache kneeling on the floor
and looking through an ancient box stuffed with
letters. 'I don't know how you can do it,' I told
him shudderingly. 'I'm looking for stamps,' he
replied. 'There's some been pinched already,
stamps worth at least a fiver, stamps before the
Penny Post came in. All pinched!' I had a picture of somebody creeping into that awful little
house, groping through that box, looking for old
stamps. Nearly all the things in the house were
good. On the ground floor were dusty shapes that
were discovered on examination to be charming
old chairs, a spinet, bow-fronted chests of
drawers, inlaid card tables, and the like. But it

was the chief bedroom, where the women were so busy turning things over, that was most fascinating. On a fine four-poster bed were laid out exquisite old dresses and shawls and bundles of unused linen sheets. It was like finding fresh flowers in a dustbin. I heard some talk of wedding dresses. One was spread out, lighting up the room, a lovely shimmer of fabric. This, I was told, was a gem: a crinoline of silver and lilac brocade. There were other crinolines too, nearly as beautiful: green striped taffeta with black lace appliqué —so ran the expert description. The women there, forgetting the dust and their skirts and the spiders, turned over these and other garments and gave little cries of astonishment and delight. I had a sudden vision of a girl in the 'fifties, a very happy girl, pirouetting in these things before the mirror, trying this and trying that, wondering whether he would like her best in lilac and silver. There were some leather cases on top of a chest of drawers, and when I opened them they seemed at first to be nothing but slightly discoloured pieces of glass. But when I looked again, faces from a past age, girls with side-curls, whiskered young gentlemen with immense cravats, smiling or puzzled children, looked out at me. Probably among these faded daguerreotypes were several portraits of *him*, who would come down, like a whiskered and cravated god, to choose between the silver and lilac brocade and the green striped taffeta.

Yes, she had been a happy girl. Those vague faces of the daguerreotypes were once a host of approving relatives, smiling friends. And nobody had more luxuriant whiskers or cravats than he, who had said, again and again, that he loved her. And where could you find prettier dresses and shawls? Were not the very sheets the finest linen? There had been moments, probably when she was turning over these things just as the women were turning them over yesterday morning, when she had seen life stretching before her like a high road through one great golden valley. She had only to live on, just to breathe, to be happier and happier. And then, and then—dust, and more dust, first a grey film of it, and at last inches of black grime.

Do I imagine all this to be very romantic? I do. Do I know that I am being very sentimental? I do. Does it occur to me that I am merely a sentimental literary man who is not only embroidering but probably grossly distorting the facts? No, it doesn't, by Jingo! As I went through that little horror of a house yesterday, I learned some of the facts, and here they are and you can make of them what you will.

This house had been shut up for years. Its owner had lived there alone for a long period, and by the time she was middle-aged she was probably known to be cranky, eccentric, perhaps a little mad. I heard one woman, herself middle-aged, say yesterday: 'She chased me many a time'; and I had a vision of this solitary woman, with the queer and even sinister reputation, running out of her remote little house to chase away the children who came to explore the fringes of the garden, climb the walls, and make faces at her. When she was past eighty she began to fail and at last had to be removed, filthy, horribly neglected, to the local workhouse infirmary, where finally she died, in her 'nineties. It was then discovered that she had been by no means penniless, as everybody imagined, but possessed a little fortune, something in the neighbourhood of ten thousand pounds. It is clear that she was a miser. But that is not why she kept all the crinolines, the lilac and silver brocade, the green striped taffeta, in which she would have peacocked through her honeymoon. Apparently the wedding was all arranged and then she was jilted. In fact, we have here another Miss Havisham. And those who like irony will enjoy the sequel to this old-fashioned story. There were the ten thousand pounds and this house and its furniture, and an heir had to be found. At last he was found, and he proved to be a rich American, who has recently been cruising the Mediterranean in his own yacht. When he was told about the furniture he is reported to have said: 'Sell the lot. I don't care what it fetches.'

So, yesterday morning, the antique furniture and household effects of Lilac Cottage were—like life—on view.

IT WAS easily done. First, we walked through the village, which is nothing but one long winding street. Now and then we stopped to look at a doorway or a bit of garden. This is a stone village and its walls are its art gallery. Weather and the lichens have sketched in some masterpieces, and the sunlight did the rest. It is a beautiful village. But where are the rosy-cheeked and clear-eyed villagers in this island of ours? Have they vanished with the smock? The women we saw in those delightful doorways were nearly all dark slatterns who would have looked at home in the nearest city slums. They have greasy locks and long sallow faces. Their appearance suggested gin and fried fish. And the children like apples, where were they?

It is the habit of theatrical managers to buy the scenery and effects of some London revue, and then send it on tour with a fifth-rate company, worlds away from the original cast, the ingenious buffoons, the clever dancers and the rows of pretty girls, who entertained the West End. Rural England, these days, is like one of those touring productions. The original scenery and effects are still there, the most lavish 'sets' and charming backcloths; but the people playing in front of them are all wrong. What has become of the old cast, the bright blue eyes and ruddy cheeks, the stalwart men, the red-lipped girls, and the angelic children?

We do not pause for a reply. We are not concerned with the village. Our business is to get out of it, out of everything, as the two of us did the other morning. We had time to see the sunlight creep along the old walls, and then we walked out of the village. The road narrowed and climbed, became in fact a kind of terrace, bordered by pines on one side and little sycamores, still bare and delicate, on the other. Now the sunshine struggled down to us through a light mist, which obscured the hills. From the right there came a crackling sound, then a smell of burning. We turned up a narrow lane, walked forward for a few yards, and stared up at the ghostly hill-side. Dim ribbons of flame were fluttering there: they were burning the undergrowth somewhere on the hill. It cleared a little and we saw the flames leap up, higher and higher. Oh, if it would only burn the whole hill, go roaring to the sky! We waited wistfully for some vast conflagration, the incendiary or salamander that lives on in the hearts of all of us, gleeful at the sight of every new writhing tassel of flame and sulky at once whenever the orange tongues dwindled and finally disappeared in clouds of smoke.

A turn of the road brought us into Roman Italy. That is really the most delightful thing about England. You never know—could never guess—what is waiting for you round the corner. Eccentric aristocrats have worked their wills on this island for centuries, with the result that anything may happen in it. Some time during the eighteenth century, the local lord of the manor here paid a visit to Italy, returning with a head humming with eclogues and Virgilian tags and plans for improving the estate. Thus we walked into Roman Italy. But first we rested on it; that is, we found a carved stone seat at the side of the road, antique Italy in every line and crevice of it, and sat there in the vague trembling sunlight. After that, for the next half mile or so, England disappeared. We moved in a tiny world of sharp light and shadow, of grave dark beauty, of fine lines and harsh surfaces. Virgil himself could have

paced that ilex-bordered avenue at ease, waiting
for the magic of his thunder and tears. Here and
there, between the dark trees, were great clumps
of some gigantic alien grass, pale yellow and as
dry as new matches. I do not know what this
grass was. It may not have been Italian, but it
certainly was not English. If a leopard had suddenly poked its head out of that blanched rustling
stuff, I should not have been surprised.

The road now turned a sharp corner and ran
sharply down—into nothing. Classical Italy had
gone, but England had not reappeared. There
were, of course, a few sights and sounds. Some
doves were crooning somewhere, perhaps just on
the rim of the world. We saw a fantastically
coloured bird that had just hopped out of a
Chinese drawing. It was, we knew, a pheasant,
delicately reared so that red-faced men in Harris
tweed coats might blow the life out of it in a
few months' time; but at the moment it was impossible to believe in the existence of those men
and their Diamond smokeless powder; the bird
was there, fresh from the hand of some almond-
eyed water-colourist. Then, in the dip at the bot-
tom, on the last few yards of grass, a cow was
grazing, a solid English cow. It is true that at

first I was not astonished to see the cow. But then I had not noticed the boats. For, in front of us, above this dip, was a little hill, the top of which ran straight across the horizon. There was nothing to be seen before us but the vague mass, a faint gold, of this unusual little hill. And then as we walked towards it I noticed that some dark shapes on its slope suddenly turned themselves into beached boats. You cannot have boats on a hill-side, even though everything is becoming queer. I looked at the cow and I looked again at the boats. There was nothing else to see, but that was quite enough. Something was wrong or everything was going quietly, stealthily, mad.

We left the cow behind and began to climb this hill. Immediately our feet sank and floundered. We were treading on pebbles, thousands and thousands of tiny pebbles. The whole hill was made of pebbles. We could hear a noise, a steady rustling noise. Plunging away, we mounted the crest, and at once the whole day became brighter and we looked down upon a vague glitter. 'Roosh-sh-sh-arsh,' it said, this creaming line of water, sucking away at the pebbles. We descended to another crest, and immediately the 'Roosh-sh-sh-arsh' grew louder. We looked to left and right. On each side the bank of pebbles stretched out until it was lost to sight in a dwindling brightness of spray and mist. In front the sea curved and curdled, swayed and glittered, then mounted to the sky and was there indistinguishably mingled with vapour and uneasy sunlight. It was all a great emptiness.

The long wave broke like soft thunder and then harshly swept back the tiny pebbles, but beyond that, nothing happened. Not a boat went sailing; not a black fin moved; not a single sea-bird flashed and cried in the vacant air. We struggled on a little farther, and saw the delicate pattern of the pebbles broken in one place by what seemed a piece of black wood. It moved a little. We went nearer, and then it became a bird standing erect. It was dressed like an old shabby clerk, in black that had a green sheen on it. When we were only a few yards away, it turned and looked at us, then waddled towards the water, shaking itself rather indignantly. Even then, we would not let it alone; so, with a last indignant or contemptuous flutter, it suddenly dived straight into the breaker, just where the water turns a magical pale green. A minute or two later it bobbed up, now several yards out, and allowed itself to be carried ashore again. Then it dived again, and we lost sight of it. Thereafter, it seemed, we had Chesil Bank to ourselves.

When you lie down at full length and see them close, those pebbles are enchanting. They have every colour and every combination of colours, and you can spend hours and hours collecting black ones with red stripes or cream ones banded with brown, and all you have to do, to bring up a fresh assortment, is to sweep your hand across the top and then begin collecting again. Ali Baba in his cave had no richer profusion of stones. The sun scattered the last shreds of mist and smote the south ridge of the bank so strongly that you could see the shimmer of heat above the pebbles. The whole land disappeared, but sent a singing lark to remind us it was still there somewhere. Ours was a world of sun, air, water, pebbles, and this mad trilling in the blue. Nobody came. Nothing happened. For a few hours we were out of it, gloriously out of it, living richly on a current account in Chesil Bank.